Project editor Lizzie Davey
Project art editor Fiona Macdonald
Editor Ann Baggaley
US editor Margaret Parrish
Senior producer, pre-production Luca Frassinetti
Producer Mary Slater
Jacket designer Laura Brim
Jacket coordinator Maud Whatley
Jacket design development manager Sophia MTT
Managing editor Paula Regan
Managing art editor Owen Peyton Jones
Publisher Sarah Larter
Art director Phil Ormerod
Associate publishing director Liz Wheeler
Publishing director Jonathan Metcalf

DK Delhi
Senior editor Sreshtha Bhattacharya
Senior art editor Anjana Nair
Assistant editor Tejaswita Payal
Project art editor Neha Sharma
Art editors Ankita Mukherjee, Devan Das, Namita
Assistant art editors Roshni Kapur, Vansh Kohli
Jacket designer Suhita Dharamjit
Jacket editorial manager Saloni Talwar
Senior DTP jacket designer Harish Aggarwal
Managing editor Pakshalika Jayaprakash
Managing art editor Arunesh Talapatra
Production manager Pankaj Sharma
Pre-production manager Balwant Singh
DTP designers Anita Yadav, Syed Md Farhan
Picture researchers Deepak Negi,
Surya Sankash Sarangi
Picture research manager Taiyaba Khatoon

Authors Sarah Tomley, Marcus Weeks

First American Edition, 2015
Published in the United States by DK Publishing
345 Hudson Street, New York, New York 10014

Copyright © 2015 Dorling Kindersley Limited
A Penguin Random House Company
15 16 17 18 19 10 9 8 7 6 5 4 3 2 1
001—266552—March 2015

A catalog record for this book is available from the Library of Congress.
ISBN 978-1-4654-2923-0

DK books are available at special discounts when purchased in bulk for sales promotions, premiums, fund-raising, or educational use. For details, contact: DK Publishing Special Markets, 345 Hudson Street, New York, New York 10014
SpecialSales@dk.com

Printed and bound in Hong Kong

www.dk.com

Children's BOOK OF Philosophy

An introduction to the world's
great thinkers and their big ideas

Contents

86 How do I decide what's right?

116 Why do we need rules?

"Philosophy is not a theory, but an activity."

—Ludwig Wittgenstein

What is philosophy?

WHEN did philosophy BEGIN?

Philosophy began thousands of years ago, when people first questioned the meaning of life and how the world was made. The earliest philosophers we know about lived in ancient Greece in around 600 BCE.

How do philosophers teach?

Philosophers ask the kinds of questions that science can't answer—for instance, "Why is there a world?" They encourage their students to start asking questions themselves, instead of taking everything for granted or accepting what other people say.

Are all philosophers old men with beards?

Many early Greek philosophers did have beards, but they certainly weren't all old—although some spent a lifetime teaching. Many of them attracted a huge following of young fans. Today, women and men of all ages are philosophers.

Can I be a PHILOSOPHER?

If you are curious about the world and enjoy asking questions, you are probably already well on your way to being a philosopher. You don't have to go to school or take tests, unless you want to. You can simply enjoy using your mind.

Philosophy means "love of wisdom." It is a method of trying to **understand ourselves and our world by asking a lot of questions**. Philosophers spend a great deal of time thinking, wondering, talking, and listening.

Questions!
What about *answers?*

Philosophers have all kinds of different ways of tackling tricky questions. Sometimes they find an answer, but often philosophical questions don't have answers. The important thing is to continue trying to discover the truth.

WHY should *I learn* philosophy?

Philosophy can teach you to think more clearly and to be confident in debates and discussions. It may even help you to make decisions about how you want to live.

Isn't *philosophy* a little *weird?*

It's true that philosophical questions can sound slightly crazy—for example, "Am I real?" or "Is color just in the mind?" But questions like these show that philosophers are trying to find out what's really going on in the world and in ourselves.

Should I TRY out philosophy *with friends?*

Philosophy is definitely for sharing. It can be lots of fun talking about ideas and exchanging thoughts with your friends. You'll probably find they think about things very differently than you do, which is a great starting point.

Is the *world* **real?**

from? **Are the things in it real or are they just thoughts in our minds?**

What *is the* world *made of?*

The ancient Greeks were the first people to really think about how and why the world was made and where everything in it, living and nonliving, came from. Some of their ideas—for example, that our world was originally built from water, air, or mud— are very easy to understand. But other ideas are so complicated that even today philosophers debate exactly what they mean.

Water

Thales (c.625–545 BCE) believed that the world developed from just one thing: water. He could see that water changed into mist, steam, and ice, and he thought that this shifting could explain how things in the world change. Thales even thought that our planet floated on water. An old story about Thales pokes fun at him for being so busy wondering what was happening in heaven that he didn't look where he was going and fell down a well.

Air

Anaximenes of Miletus (c.585–525 BCE) had the idea that our world was created out of thin air. He thought that in the beginning there was nothing but air, which gradually got thicker and changed into other things. First, winds started to blow, then the air became visible as clouds, then it grew more and more solid, turning into water, soil, stones, and everything else.

Anaximenes at work

Mud and mist

Anaximander of Miletus (c.611–547 BCE) agreed with Thales that everything in the world developed from one substance, but he didn't think it was water. He believed it was mud and mist that was left behind as water on the newly developing Earth steamed away under the heat of the Sun. He also decided that something else was needed as well. Anaximander didn't describe exactly what this mystery ingredient was, but he said it was unlimited and that it made the four basic elements of earth, water, air, and fire.

The unchanging "One"

According to Parmenides (born c.510 BCE) everything in the world counts as a single thing. This "One," as he called it, can't be divided into different parts and never changes. Of course, we do see things changing, but Parmenides said this is just our senses playing tricks on us. His ideas led to a lot of discussion among philosophers, especially his suggestion that there is no such thing as "nothing."

Parmenides

Constant change

Heraclitus (c.540–480 BCE) found that the problem with trying to understand the world was that it keeps changing all the time. He famously remarked that you cannot step twice into the same river. What he meant was that by the time you take the second step, the river has flowed on, so even just one second later the water is different. Heraclitus suggested that behind everything that exists there is a universal law or master plan. Although we can't see or sense this, it controls our lives.

Four elements

The theory that everything is made of four basic materials, or elements—earth, water, air, and fire—was popular in ancient Greece. Empedocles of Acragas (c.495–435 BCE) supported this idea. First, he claimed, fire threw up formless lumps. Then, as the elements became mixed up in endless ways, the lumps turned into all the things we recognize, such as rocks, plants, animals, and people. Empedocles thought the elements were controlled by two powerful forces: love and strife, or disagreement.

Tiny building blocks

Like many other early Greeks, Leucippus (c.500 BCE) and his student Democritus (c.470–380 BCE) thought that whatever the world was made from it had to be just one thing. They decided that this must be the tiniest of all building blocks, a scrap too small to be divided into smaller parts. Leucippus called it an atom, explaining that all things were made of atoms clumped together in different ways.

Extra special

Aristotle (384–322 BCE) wanted to know how living things came to exist, what they were for, and why they are different from nonliving objects. He thought anything alive had a mysterious extra something inside that was different from the body itself. Aristotle called this the "psyche"; today, many people call it the mind and it still seems magical. People continue to argue today about Aristotle's idea. Is the mind just part of the body? Or is it an entirely separate thing?

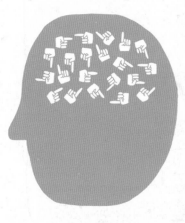

Why is there something *rather than* nothing?

After thinking about what the world was made of, the ancient Greek philosophers questioned why there was a world at all. Why was there something, rather than nothing? Is it possible that **something has always existed?** We are so used to thinking of beginnings and endings that it is hard to imagine that something has always been there. On the other hand, could something such as the universe have been created from nothing?

Parmenides

There must be something

Parmenides believed that things don't just burst into existence. He said it is impossible for "things that are not" to suddenly become "things that are." Nothing can come from nothing. He also said that it doesn't make sense even to think of nothing, because we can't imagine nothing. If nothingness is impossible then there must be something.

You move faster on land than in water because water is denser.

Impossibly fast

Aristotle also believed nothingness was impossible, and he used scientific reasons to support his argument. He said that the speed with which something moves through a medium—such as water—depends on how dense it is. But nothingness would have no density, so things would move infinitely fast, which is impossible!

What came first?

When we ask "Why is something here?" we normally mean "What caused this?" For example, if you were asked about why you are here, you might say that you are here because of your parents. And they are here because of your grandparents, and so on. Aristotle thought that there must be something at the beginning of the whole human chain, and even the universe itself, that was not caused by anything else. He believed this "first cause" was God.

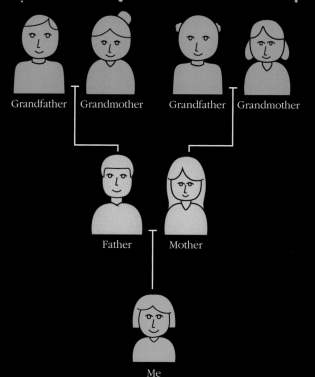

Grandfather | Grandmother | Grandfather | Grandmother

Father | Mother

Me

If you look at your family tree backward—starting with you—then eventually you will find your first ancestors. But who created them?

Story of the universe

Scientists say that the universe started with a Big Bang—a powerful explosion—that caused everything else to grow into existence. So that would mean that Earth did not come from nothing—it came about because of the Big Bang. But what caused the Big Bang? Scientists and philosophers say that it is impossible for there to be absolutely nothing. So perhaps before the Big Bang there were just tiny vibrations. But what caused them?

Scientists believe our universe was formed around 14 billion years ago. But what formed it?

Beyond physics

In philosophy, questions about what exists are grouped together under the term "metaphysics." The word means "after physics" because one of Aristotle's early works about physics sparked debates about existence. Today, we think of it as all the kinds of things that go beyond or above the physical and that can't be answered by physics. Questions such as "Why is there something rather than nothing?" and "Is there a god?" are metaphysical questions.

Ideas of nothingness

Henri Bergson

French philosopher Henri Bergson said that nothingness was impossible. Even in space, an astronaut must sense something, even if that is just blackness. Bergson said that if we met with a completely empty space it would have to be contained, so it would have edges, giving it a shape. But if a space has edges and a shape, it is something, not nothing. There is, therefore, no such thing as "nothing."

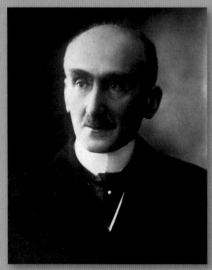

Henri Bergson (1859–1941)

Always something

Bergson said that humans start with nothing, then start looking for things that they need—food, shelter, and so on. We make the mistake of imagining that the whole world works in the same way—starting with nothing. But the world does not "think" like a human being—there is always "something" and never "nothing."

What is nothing?

For thousands of years philosophers have argued about what exists. Could it be that nothing at all exists? Part of the problem is that **we cannot imagine "nothing,"** since there is nothing to imagine! Is there such a thing as "nothing"? How can we describe or imagine a lack of anything at all? American philosopher Robert Nozick asks us to try to think it through, using the following example.

Nozick said that for there to be nothing, there must be something making that nothing happen by keeping no object or person there. He asks us to imagine a huge vacuum cleaner that goes around vacuuming everything up. Eventually there is nothing left but the vacuum cleaner itself. For there to be nothing at all, the vacuum cleaner must then vacuum itself up. At this point, however, it will have sucked "nothingness" into nothingness, and when there is no longer any "nothing," there must be "something."

If we ask "Why is there something rather than nothing?" it sounds as if we think "nothing" is the natural way for things to be, and "something" is a step on from this. But maybe it is more natural for there to be things, rather than for there to be nothing? If so, we do not have to wonder about why there is something, because it is natural for something to exist.

If a black hole sucked everything in until there was nothing left, would it also suck in itself?

Think about it!

The meaning of "nothing"

Some philosophers say that when we talk about "nothing," we are not really talking about a lack of anything at all. We are talking about "something," but something other than what we were looking for. For instance, if we were to say that "Jane is not tall," it does not mean Jane has no tallness, or no height. It just means that Jane is something other than tall. She may be short or of average height. Similarly, when we use the word "nothing" it is wrong to think that the word refers to a total vacuum.

"Something" is more likely

Probability looks at how likely something is. For example, children go to school five days of the week when school is in session, and on just two days a week they do not go to school. If someone were to stick a pin in a calendar showing the school year, they would be more likely to hit a school day than a weekend.

In the same way, Nozick said, it's more likely for something to exist than for nothing to exist at all, because there are many possible worlds of something, but only one possible world of nothing. He compared it to having a huge sack of red balls (these are all the possible "something" worlds) and adding just one white ball (the "nothing" world) to the sack: Isn't the chance of pulling out a red ball much higher? That's the chance of there being something.

Biography

c.470 BCE Born in Athens, Greece, the son of a stonemason whose trade he at first followed.

c.445 BCE Drafted for military service in the Athenian army.

c.435 BCE Marries Xanthippe, with whom he will have three sons.

c.424 BCE Takes part in a battle against the Spartans at Delium.

c.423 BCE Portrayed as a comic character in a new play called *The Clouds* by the Athenian writer Aristophanes.

c.407 BCE Meets the philosopher Plato, who will later record Socrates' ideas in his own works.

399 BCE Accused of not believing in the gods and corrupting the young people of Athens. Found guilty and sentenced to death. Executed by being made to swallow poison.

Favorite student
Of all the students that Socrates taught, the one he favored most was a rich, spoiled young aristocrat named Alcibiades. Socrates is said to have saved Alcibiades' life in battle, when they were both in the Athenian army fighting against Sparta. They remained friends for life, even though they lived their lives in very different ways. Alcibiades became a powerful politician and does not seem to have lived up to Socrates' ideal of putting goodness before wealth and fame.

Socrates

*"I cannot teach anybody anything.
I can only make them think."*

Born around 470 BCE, Socrates was a Greek who lived in Athens during the city-state's cultural golden age. He stood out among other great thinkers of the time because of his new way of asking questions. His style became known as the Socratic method. Despite Socrates' great influence on philosophy, he left no written work behind. We know about him only through the work of other people, such as the philosopher Plato.

The wisest man

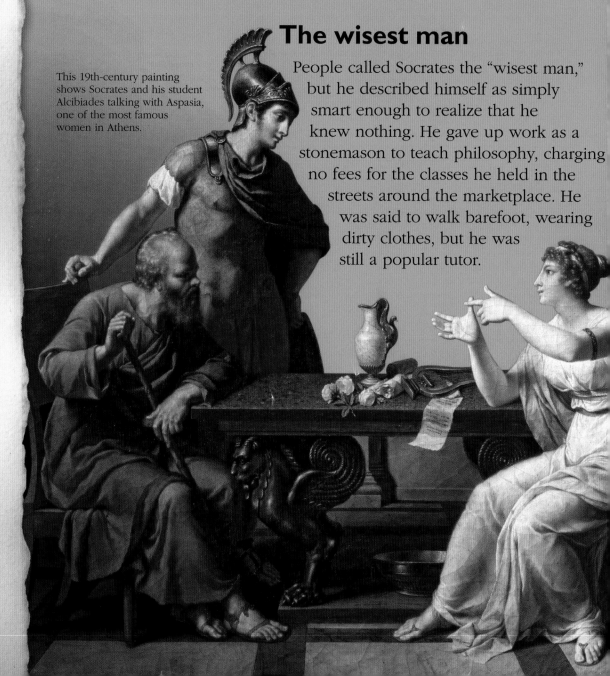

This 19th-century painting shows Socrates and his student Alcibiades talking with Aspasia, one of the most famous women in Athens.

People called Socrates the "wisest man," but he described himself as simply smart enough to realize that he knew nothing. He gave up work as a stonemason to teach philosophy, charging no fees for the classes he held in the streets around the marketplace. He was said to walk barefoot, wearing dirty clothes, but he was still a popular tutor.

What is true?

All philosophers agree with Socrates' belief that we need to find out the true meaning of things. We should not always accept what people tell us. Nor should we take it for granted that what we say and think is true. If we talk about love or anger, for example, do we really understand what we are saying? Socrates thought the best way to get at the truth of anything was to keep asking questions.

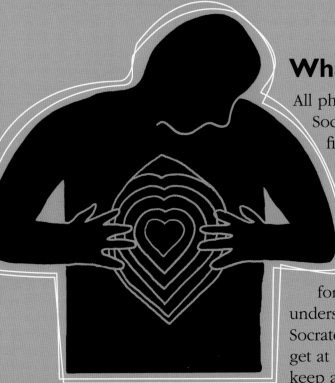

How do we know what love is?

How should we live?

What makes a good life?—that was the most important question for Socrates. Most people of his time would have chosen fame, money, and power, but these things didn't interest Socrates. He thought that we should forget about personal comfort and possessions and pursue the truth. We must work out what "good" really means and try to do the right things. Socrates said people were not bad on purpose, but did bad things only because they didn't know better.

To Socrates, trying to make other people happy was an important part of living a good life.

The death of Socrates

As his students weep, Socrates drinks the poison that will kill him.

In 399 BCE, Socrates was accused of disrespect to the Athenian gods and also of putting wrong ideas into the minds of young people. Rather than flee to avoid trial, he decided to defend himself instead. The jury found him guilty and he was condemned to either exile or death. Socrates chose death, and 30 days after his trial he was executed by being given the poison hemlock to drink. He is said to have taken this cheerfully, saying that he would either have a dreamless sleep or find himself having interesting conversations in the underworld.

A session with Socrates

Imagine sitting on a street corner in ancient Athens talking to Socrates. He would ask you a question—one to which you were sure you had the right answer. But then Socrates would ask another question, and another. Gradually, you would start to wonder if your first answer really was right after all. That was how Socrates taught people to think. A simple example of his method of questioning is shown below.

> So you think that the gods know everything?

> *Yes, because they are gods.*

> Do some gods disagree with others?

> *Yes, of course they do. They are always fighting.*

> So gods disagree about what is true and right?

> *I suppose they must.*

> So some gods can be wrong sometimes?

> *I suppose that is true.*

> Therefore, the gods cannot know everything!

Is there a god?

Ancient religions around the world took for granted that there was a god, or multiple gods. It didn't occur to most people to wonder **if there really was a god**, or whether they could prove that one exists. But philosophy is all about asking these questions. Are there good reasons to say that there is a god or higher being? How could we prove that one exists?

Who created the creator?

Aristotle (384–322 BCE) said that the universe must have been made, or caused, by something. If we look around us, we can see that everything is caused by something else. For instance, paintings only exist because someone painted them. So someone, or something, must have made the world, and that thing is often called god. But what made god? Aristotle said that God is the one thing that was not created by something else.

Zeus was the king of all the gods in the religion of the ancient Greeks.

The greatest

The idea that God is the greatest thing ever (so great that nothing could be greater) was put forward by the Italian philosopher Anselm (1033–1109). He argued that part of the reason that something is "the best" is that it actually exists. For example, an imaginary cake is not as good as a real cake. So if God is the greatest thing ever, he must exist.

The world's designer

Perhaps looking around us shows us there is a god. Everything in the world is so amazing and complex—shells have very beautiful designs, for instance, and our bodies are extremely complicated. Italian philosopher Thomas Aquinas said that looking around us proves that a great, supremely intelligent being must have made everything in the world, and this being must be God. Could the beautiful things we see in nature have been created by anything other than a great and intelligent being?

Feathers

Shell

Leaf

Does God still change things?

If there is a god who made the world, then does that mean God still changes things in the world? The Deists are a group of philosophers who believe that there is a god, but that he now lets the world go on as it is without interfering. They believe that God set up the laws of nature—such as the law that the Sun rises every day—but that God lets the world develop in its own way. So God might hear someone's prayers, but he would not step in to change anything.

Betting on God

Either God exists or he does not. French thinker Blaise Pascal (1623–62) argued that if we can't prove God exists we are better off believing in him. This is because if we believe in God, then we will go to heaven when we die. If there is not a god, it does not matter. But, if we do not believe God exists, and it turns out that he does, then we will have a lot of explaining to do when we die and meet our creator.

Pascal said it makes sense to bet on the existence of a higher being.

St. Thomas Aquinas

Thomas Aquinas was a Catholic priest and one of the most important philosophers of his time. He wrote a lot about God—especially what God is like and how God has no beginning and no end. He was also interested in how we judge people's actions to be "good" or "bad."

St. Thomas Aquinas

c.1225: Born in a hilltop castle in Naples, Italy. His parents were a count and countess.

c.1230: Goes to school in a monastery and, against his family's wishes, becomes a monk.

1243: His brothers kidnap him from the monastery and take him home, on his mother's orders. He is kept at home and is not allowed to go out until his mother changes her mind, and he rejoins the monastery.

1244–1274: Goes to Rome to study with Pope Innocent IV, then studies in France, Germany, and Italy, becoming a well-known writer and philosopher.

1274: Has a mystical experience and says he will not write anything else, because everything he had written now "looked like straw" to him. He dies three months later during a trip to see the Pope.

Biography

c.428 BCE Born in Athens, Greece, to a rich and powerful family.

c.420 BCE Meets Socrates, who influences him more than any other teacher.

c.418 BCE Studies music, poetry, and philosophy.

409–404 BCE Joins the Athenian army to fight in the Peloponnesian War between Sparta and Athens.

399 BCE Socrates is executed, and Plato leaves Greece to travel for 12 years. During this time, he studies geometry, astronomy, religion, and philosophy.

387 BCE Plato returns to Athens and opens Europe's first university, called The Academy. He starts writing his famous "dialogues" there.

367 BCE Plato is invited to be the tutor of Dionysus II, the ruler of Syracuse.

365 BCE Returns to Athens to teach at The Academy, where he meets his most famous pupil, Aristotle.

361 BCE Returns to tutor Dionysus for a while, but soon returns to The Academy, where he continues to write and teach.

Famous work

Plato wrote many plays and recorded many conversations, called "dialogues," which became very famous. Many of his works feature a character named Socrates. This character was probably based on the real Socrates, who had been a great influence on Plato. Plato went on to influence many philosophers himself, including his pupil Aristotle.

Plato

"The object of education is to teach us to love what is beautiful."

Plato is one of the **most important philosophers of the Western world**. He was one of the first philosophers to think about all kinds of important questions, such as "What is beauty?" Philosophers today still argue about many of the things Plato said more than 2,000 years ago.

The broad one

Plato's real name was Aristocles, but he was given the nickname "Platon," which means "the broad one," because his body was broad and strong. He had a good education and went on to become a soldier and then a politician. After his teacher Socrates was executed for his beliefs, Plato left Athens to travel the world. On his return, he opened The Academy, Europe's first university.

This Roman mosaic shows Plato with his students at The Academy.

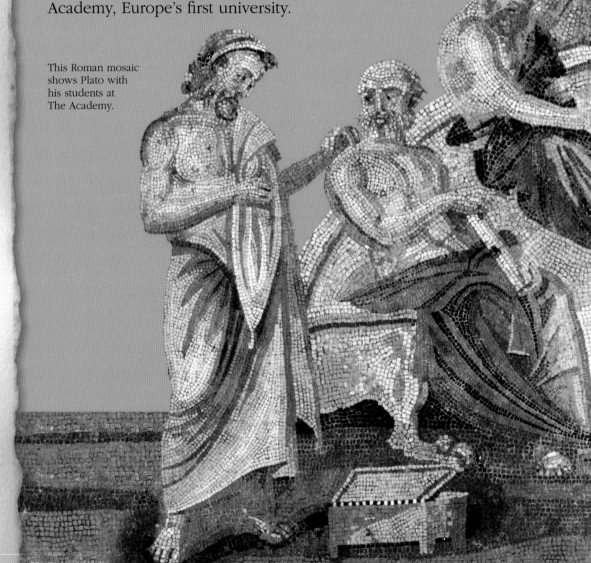

Exploring the world

During his travels, Plato visited Egypt and Italy and learned many new ideas. He had been taught that everything constantly changes, but in Italy he met the followers of Pythagoras, a great mathematician, and realized that numbers are special things that do not change. This led Plato to wonder whether there were other things, too, that did not change.

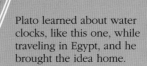

Plato learned about water clocks, like this one, while traveling in Egypt, and he brought the idea home.

Born to reason

Plato, like many of the ancient Greek philosophers, believed that we can only gain knowledge by thinking things through—by reasoning. Plato demonstrated this by telling a story about Socrates discussing a math problem with a slave boy who had never been to school. By watching Socrates drawing diagrams in the sand, the boy understood and learned how to solve the problem. Socrates had not given him the answer, but the boy knew what it was. Plato said that this story proves we are born with the power to reason, which is the source of all our knowledge.

Socrates drew diagrams in the sand to help a slave boy figure out the answers to a problem for himself.

The perfect state

In Plato's opinion, the perfect place to live would be in a group of people, so that people with different skills could help each other. To help resolve disagreements there would be soldiers to defend the people and wise rulers who would settle arguments, make good decisions, and establish laws. Plato believed these rulers should be trained as philosophers from childhood, to make sure they were good thinkers.

How can we know what exists?

If someone asked you "What exists?" you would probably point to the things around you and say "Everything!" If asked how you knew, you might answer that you can see, hear, touch, smell, or taste it all. But some philosophers think that it's not that simple. **Our senses can be tricked and they might not tell the truth.** Can we ever really know what's real?

The perfect form

The ancient Greek philosopher Plato said that there are two types of reality. One is our world, with everything we see, hear, and touch. The second is another world full of perfect things that Plato called "forms." He said that in our world we have only imperfect copies of forms that exist in another world. For instance, the dogs we see are less-than-perfect copies of the "form of dog." Plato believed that we hold the idea of perfect forms in our minds, so we can recognize the copies when we meet them.

Plato said all things are copied from ideal "forms," as statues are imperfect copies of people.

A world of shadows

This imagined scene helps explain Plato's idea of forms. Imagine a group of people who have been imprisoned in a cave since they were born. They are tied up facing the back wall of the cave, which is all they can see. Near the cave entrance there is a fire that casts shadows onto the back wall. Sometimes other people walk along a path between the fire and the cave. They hold up puppets, which appear as shadows on the cave wall. Since this is all the prisoners have ever known, they think the shadows are real objects. Plato said that we are like these prisoners. We think the things we see and hear around us are real. In fact, they are like shadows of the real things, which are the forms.

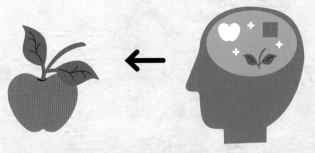

Collecting information

Plenty of later philosophers disagreed with Plato's ideas about reality. They didn't believe we need perfect forms to explain how we know things, and they suggested instead that our minds gather information. Take an apple, for example. Our senses tell us about its particular color, shape, feel, and taste. All this information is collected and organized in our minds. We see the fruit and immediately think "apple" because that's the name we have been taught.

Just an idea?

When we see, hear, or touch something, we form an idea of what it is. So when we feel something fluffy and see brownness and big ears, we might decide this adds up to the idea of a "rabbit." "Rabbit" is a human word and idea. But if "rabbit" is just an idea in your head, what do you really know? You know you have an idea, but do you really have a rabbit? And what happens if no one is around to have the idea—is there still a rabbit?

Is a rabbit on the grass only there because our minds say so? If we didn't have the idea of "rabbit," would it vanish?

Only ideas are real

Tables and tricks

The suggestion that only ideas are real is known as "idealism." It can seem very odd to ask yourself how you know something—say, a table—is there in front of you. Your senses give you information about it: it's hard, wooden, has legs, and so on. But to figure out that this object is a table you have to use reason. Try altering some of the information. If the table moved, all by itself, would you change your mind about what it is? Magicians take advantage of our ideas about what is real to perform their tricks. They say, "See this? And this? But now watch—nothing is as you thought!"

Magicians can fool us with their tricks because they know what we expect to see in a normal world.

Beyond our senses

Perhaps, as the idealist philosopher Immanuel Kant suggested, there are real things in the world outside our minds. Unfortunately, we have no way of knowing what they actually are. All we know about things comes from what we sense about them. But what if you had 10 different senses instead of just five? What would the world seem like to you then?

Aristotle

"The roots of education are bitter, but the fruit is sweet."

Biography

384 BCE Born in Stagira, a Greek colony, to parents named Phaestis and Nichomacus.

367 BCE Sent to The Academy in Athens, to study with Plato.

348 BCE On Plato's death, goes traveling. During this period meets and marries Pythias, the daughter of one of his friends.

343–40 BCE Moves to Macedonia to tutor Alexander the Great.

335 BCE Founds his own school, The Lyceum, in Athens.

323 BCE Flees when Athens turns against him because of his links with Alexander. He settles in Chalcis on the island of Euboea.

322 BCE Dies at age 63 of a digestive illness.

Writings saved
For a long time, Aristotle's writings were kept at his school, The Lyceum. Some of them were destroyed by damp and pests, but others were rediscovered in 100 BCE and moved to Rome. Here, they were published and much admired. Centuries later, in the Middle Ages, Aristotle's works again became very important to philosophers in both the East and West.

Possibly **the most important philosopher who ever lived**, Aristotle made a difference to people all over the world. A great scholar, he knew a lot about a huge number of things, from math, biology, physics, and medicine, to farming and theater. He showed people how to use reason to work things out in a systematic way. Aristotle wrote about 200 short books, but only around 30 have survived.

Learning from Plato

Aristotle grew up in royal surroundings in the ancient kingdom of Macedonia, where his father was a court doctor. At the age of 17, Aristotle was sent to study in Athens with Plato, the most famous teacher of the time. Aristotle stayed at Plato's Academy for more than 20 years, both as a student and a teacher. He was such a brilliant student that people thought he might become head of The Academy when Plato died. But because Aristotle and Plato disagreed over some important things, the position went to Plato's nephew instead.

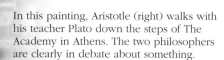
In this painting, Aristotle (right) walks with his teacher Plato down the steps of The Academy in Athens. The two philosophers are clearly in debate about something.

This is how a Victorian painter imagined Aristotle's school in Athens, with students gathered together in informal groups for lively discussions.

Aristotle's Lyceum

When he returned to Athens after his travels, Aristotle started his own school, The Lyceum. He gave morning classes to his pupils and lectured to the public in the afternoon. Aristotle taught history and science as well as philosophy. He liked to wander along with his students as he taught them how to think, reason, and debate.

1 **What is it made of?**

2 **What is the final design?**

3 **How was it made?**

4 **What is its purpose?**

The four causes

According to Aristotle, everything has four causes—reasons why things are the way they are. For each object, we must ask: "What is it made of?"; "What is the final design?"; "How was it made?"; and—most importantly for Aristotle—"What is its purpose?" For the four causes of a house, we can say it is made of wood, to an architect's design, put up by construction workers, to be a family home. It is not just a collection of wood and bricks— it has structure, design, and purpose as well.

Really real?

Aristotle's teacher, Plato, thought that the things in our world were not real, but instead were copies of objects that were somewhere else. His student disagreed. Aristotle said we know what's real from our experiences, and by thinking things through. For example, we understand what a frog is because we've seen lots of frogs. We recognize their size, legs, skin, and so on—the things that make up a frog.

Aristotle said that we recognize things because we see the parts they are made of.

Is color *in the* mind *or in the* object?

We see the world in color—sky, trees, houses, animals, clothes, flowers, and everything else. But **philosophers are not sure what color is or where it comes from**, and some doubt that it is there at all. Is color part of the objects we see, or something that happens entirely in our minds? Is a lemon really yellow, or does it just seem yellow to us?

Modern science teaches us that the more we study a subject the more we will understand it. But is learning facts all we need to do to gain knowledge? Some philosophers think that the most important thing is what we sense about an object. Imagine that you knew every single scientific fact about the colors of the rainbow. Would that be enough to let you know what these colors are really like, and how they make you feel?

Philosopher Frank Jackson suggested that we imagine a scientist named Mary who is an expert on the subject of how our eyes see color. She has read hundreds of books and papers and conducted lots of experiments. She appears to know everything there is to know about why colors are the way they are and what happens in people's brains when they see them. But, strangely, she has never experienced color herself. All her life she has lived in a room where everything is either black or white. So does she really know everything about color? Suppose she were taken out of her black-and-white room and placed in a world where all around her were wonderful colors. Wouldn't she gasp and be amazed? Wouldn't she learn something new beyond all the scientific information—for example, how color can have a powerful effect on what people are thinking and feeling?

If someone lived only in a black-and-white world, could they ever know everything there is to know about color?

How do we know that this lemon is yellow? Is our mind creating the idea of yellow?

When color isn't there

Many important philosophers through the centuries have believed that tastes, colors, and smells are all in the mind. According to these great thinkers, a person eating, looking, and sniffing experiences things that don't truly exist. For example, if you look at a lemon, you will perhaps see it as yellow, but if you aren't looking at the lemon is the "yellowness" still there? How can this be explained? Perhaps something happens between the lemon and our minds, so that our eyes falsely tell us the fruit is a color.

Think about it!

The question of sound
If a tree falls in the forest and there's no one there to hear it, does it make a sound? For centuries, philosophers have been debating the answer to this question. First, we need to think about the meaning of the word "sound." When something moves, it makes invisible airwaves, and our ears pick up this movement. This seems simple enough to understand—but further thinking is needed here. When our ears catch the disturbance in the airwaves, they pass the information to the brain. We need the brain to make sense of the information coming in from our ears to figure out what is going on. The processing of the airwaves happens in the mind, not in the world around us. So, if there isn't a mind to create the sound, does the falling tree really make a sound?

Should we believe our senses?
Philosophers argue that the information we receive from seeing, hearing, touching, smelling, and tasting doesn't give us true knowledge about the world. Just because we hear something it doesn't mean that it is a "true" sound. The sound messages sent to our brain depend on our measuring tools—the ears. If those ears were made differently, who knows what they might tell us. Is what I hear the same as what you hear, or what an animal hears?

Mind triggers
John Locke suggested that objects have two kinds of qualities, or special features. He called the first type primary qualities. These are things like shape and size, which he said were "built into" the object. Then he described secondary qualities, things like color or smell, that trigger a reaction in your brain, so that when you see a lemon a part of your mind immediately gets the idea of "yellow."

We don't have to stop and think about the color of a lemon. The sight of the fruit triggers a sense of "yellow" in our mind.

29

What *is* real?

Philosophers have always argued about what is real. Some believe that only ideas are real—these philosophers are known as Idealists. Realists say that only the objects around us are real. Another group of philosophers, the Pragmatists, believe that what matters is not the answer to "What is real?"—instead, what matters is what we believe to be real. They argue that **what is true is what works**.

You believe that eating cold food too quickly can hurt because it gives you a headache.

Useful beliefs

Pragmatists say that whether a belief is true or not depends on what happens if someone acts on that belief. For instance, if you believe that boiling water is very hot and that you could burn your hand if you touch it, you will stay safe. But if you believed the alternative—that boiling water is cold—and acted on that belief, your hand would get burned. Therefore, your beliefs are based on your experience. These ideas were first put forward by US philosopher Charles Peirce in 1878.

Making sense of the world

William James, a philosophy professor at Harvard University, said that pragmatism isn't really a theory—it is more like a tool that we can use to make sense of the world. Instead of looking back to what might have made something happen, it looks forward to future consequences, helping us to make decisions. For example, your beliefs about pollution and climate change might help you decide whether to buy a huge new car or a smaller one that uses less fuel.

William James (1842–1910)

We can see that the air inside the balloon is hot, making it rise up. Therefore, it is true that the air is hot.

Judging by effects

A pragmatist would say that when we talk about something, we are really looking at its effect on the world. For example, if we say something is "very hot," we are saying that it will make our senses react in a certain way. We decide whether a statement such as "the air is hot" is true by seeing what its effect on people and objects is.

Truth changes

Not all philosophers agree with the pragmatists. They believe that what is true is true, no matter what. However, judging things by their effect is much more practical—even scientific "truths" change. Many years ago, doctors believed that infections were caused by "bad air," but now they know the real cause is germs.

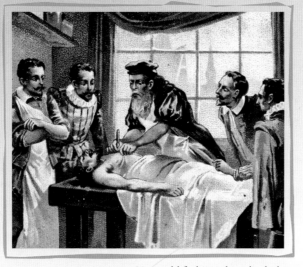

Many old-fashioned medical ideas are now known to be untrue.

Modern pragmatism

Who needs the truth?

Pragmatism was not very popular in the later part of the 20th century, until it received a big boost from American philosopher Richard Rorty. Rorty said that modern philosophy had become so caught up in trying to find the root of things, and the exact meaning of various words, that it had forgotten what the whole point of philosophy is. He asked us to look at what philosophy should do, and suggested that it is meant to help people make sense of their lives. We don't need to understand everything—just some things.

Richard Rorty (1931–2007)

A world of change

Rorty said that the world we live in is not made up of things that are true, no matter what anyone thinks or feels about them. Instead, he said our lives are made up from all the things we see, hear, feel, think, imagine, and so on. Rorty described the world we live in as being like an ongoing conversation. The world flows—things happen and affect one another so more things happen— and we are a part of that. Our days are made up of changes. We can never step outside of ourselves to find some real truth that is "out there," so why even look for it?

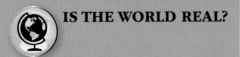

Discovering the truth

Seeing things happen

We sometimes make up our minds about the truth in the same way that researchers come to a decision about an experiment. If the same thing happens over and over again, we start thinking it must always be like this. We see the Sun rise every day and believe it will continue to do so—even if no one has explained why this is the case.

Learning from experience

Our experiences are an important part of how we learn truths about the world around us. By interacting with the world, we discover what different things are, how they work, and how they react to us. For example, we learn that snow is cold and wet, and that fish live in water.

If you prick your finger on a cactus once, you know that the next time you touch it you will be pricked again.

What *makes* *something* **true?**

We often decide what is true and what isn't true by looking back at things that have happened in the past. For example, you might say you know for sure that ice is slippery because you have fallen on ice before. Your belief seems to be true. But could it be wrong? **Believing and knowing can be two different things.**

Sometimes we have really good reasons for believing that something is true—but even so, we can still be wrong. American philosopher Edmund Gettier (1927–) said that although such a belief may turn out to be right, it wouldn't necessarily count as "knowledge." The following story explains what Gettier means.

Two school friends, Ben and Sam, have entered a race. Ben thinks Sam is likely to win, because their teacher says he is the best runner in the class. Ben also knows that Sam has three pieces of candy in his pocket. So Ben believes that the boy who has three pieces of candy in his pocket will win the race.

Surprisingly, Sam does not win; Ben does. But then Ben discovers that he has three pieces of candy in his pocket, too. His belief that the boy who will win has three pieces of candy in his pocket is true.

But although Ben turned out to be right in believing the winner had three pieces of candy, it was not knowledge. The winner of the race might not have had three pieces of candy. It was just chance that both Ben and Sam had the same amount of candy in their pockets. So, Ben was right, but his belief was not the same thing as knowledge.

The cow-in-a-field story

Imagine that a farmer is wondering whether his black-and-white cow, Daisy, is in the field. He believes she is when he goes to look, because he sees something black-and-white in the distance. Later, it turns out that what he saw was a large black-and-white bag, not Daisy. But the cow really was in the field—she was just hidden from sight in a dip. The farmer was right that Daisy was there, but wrong in what he saw. So, he didn't have real knowledge—it was just a belief that turned out to be true.

Think about it!

Truth and coincidence

We often put things together in our heads when really they have absolutely nothing to do with each other. For example, if two things happened at once we might think one caused the other, but we wouldn't necessarily be right. If it rained for seven days in a row whenever you put on your boots to go outside, you might say "Every time I want to play outside, it starts to rain." That wouldn't be true. It would just be chance—in other words, a coincidence.

Testing the truth

To test our belief in the truth of something we should look for similar things that might prove us wrong. Perhaps we think all sheep are white, for example—until we see a black sheep. Then we know that sheep can be black as well as white. We can truthfully say all sheep are white only if it is impossible for them to be any other color. But how could we ever see all the sheep in the world?

Is scientific knowledge true knowledge?

Scientists repeat their experiments many times. They think that if they nearly always get the same result, then the idea they are testing is true. But in long experiments, there are often some odd or unexpected results. Scientists ignore these, because they decide that a theory is true if they can prove it often enough. Is anything completely and certainly true?

Believing that a certain boy is going to win the race is not the same as knowing that he will win.

Can a belief work for everyone?

Some philosophers have decided that true things are the ones that everyone will find useful to be true. Let's return to our main story and suppose that a lot of other people besides Ben and Sam put three pieces of candy in their pockets. If they all won their races it might seem true that winners were always people carrying candy. But if some people without candy won, we would realize that it was wrong to believe in candy as a lucky charm. It would be more useful not to believe in magic candy and to look instead for other reasons why some people win races and others don't.

Can you **trust your senses?**

In our daily lives, it seems obvious that the things we can see, hear, touch, smell, and taste are really there, and we think we know a lot about them. We can see green grass, hear music, touch our clothes, smell burned toast, and taste a banana, and the world seems full and knowable. But **our senses can play tricks on us**—how much can we really trust them?

Unreliable senses

Everyone has been tricked by their senses at some point. Magicians trick us by making things appear, disappear, or float when we know that what we are seeing is actually impossible. A simple trick is all it takes to mislead your friends— peel some grapes and pass them to a blindfolded friend—will they believe that they are eyeballs? How can they know that they are grapes? Our senses are easily fooled.

In this photo it looks as if someone is holding the Eiffel Tower, but we know this can't be the case—we are being deceived by our own eyes.

The heat of a desert can make travelers hallucinate and see an oasis in the distance that isn't really there.

Seeing what's not there

If someone sees or hears something that is not there they are said to be having an "hallucination." The hallucination has nothing to do with the world outside the body—the problem is in that person's mind. For some reason, the mind seems to be receiving information, just as it would about a physical object, except that there is no object there. How do we know that we are not having hallucinations all the time?

Our senses work well enough

Some philosophers say that when it comes to the senses, the most practical way to live our lives is to believe that our senses give us good information most of the time. These philosophers are known as "pragmatists." They point out that our senses are our only tools for trying to figure out what is real in the world. Some illusions occur, but generally our senses work well.

Am I dreaming?

Perhaps nothing is the way our senses tell us. Perhaps we are actually dreaming all the time. How would we know? The world of dreams looks very much like the waking world—the trees, streets, and people all seem real. Philosophers have approached this problem in different ways. Thomas Hobbes pointed out that real life is not as crazy as dream life—for example, in real life you wouldn't be able to fly. John Locke realized that we don't feel pain in dreams—if you can feel a pinch you must be awake after all.

A pragmatist would say that if you hear music, you can trust your senses that music is being played.

What am I?

You might feel sure you know who you are—until you start wondering **how your mind and body work together**. Philosophers have many different ideas about what makes a person.

How do I know if I am real?

Wondering if you are real can lead to very strange thoughts. **Suppose you are just imagining real life?** Are your senses, like sight and touch, fooling you? Perhaps a wicked demon is trying to trick you into believing you exist. Such worrying ideas gave the 17th-century philosopher René Descartes a lot to think about. Eventually, he used his reason to figure out that he did exist.

Is anything true?

Descartes thought that philosophy was often based on things that people accepted as true without any real proof. This wasn't good enough for him. He hoped that by working out things like math problems he would discover truths about the world that no one could argue with. So he began to doubt everything, to see if he could find anything that couldn't be doubted.

Tricked by the senses

The first problem that Descartes decided to tackle was whether his eyes, ears, nose, and other sense organs could be trusted to tell him the truth. Were the things he could see, hear, feel, touch, and smell really there? The senses can easily be tricked. Spaghetti feels like a bowl of worms if you touch it without looking at it. Familiar things can look very different when seen from odd angles or at a distance. From far away, a big house looks tiny.

No one disagrees that 2 + 2 = 4; it is a mathematical truth. Descartes wanted to find similar true answers to philosophical questions.

Our senses are not always to be believed. If you stare at this picture, the colored circles seem to move. But they do not really move—the pattern is fooling our eyes.

How do we know that what we think we are doing is what we are actually doing?

Tricked by the mind

Do our minds ever trick us? Descartes asked himself "Am I really sitting by a fire, in my bathrobe, holding a piece of paper?" He thought at first that there couldn't be any doubt about it. Then he remembered how brain injuries can cause people to have false ideas about themselves. They think that they are kings, for instance, or imagine they are made of glass. If other people could be so wrong, couldn't he be thinking false things, too?

The evil demon

Then Descartes came up with a truly scary thought. What if an evil demon were trying to make him believe in things that were not real? At this point he had a breakthrough. Even if there were an evil demon, it could only fool someone if that person existed. You can't fool someone who doesn't exist. Descartes realized that as long as he had thoughts in his head, no matter what they were, he could be sure that at least one thing in the world was real—his mind. This was when he wrote the words that are now so well-known to philosophers: "I think, therefore I am."

Could an evil demon make someone believe things that aren't real?

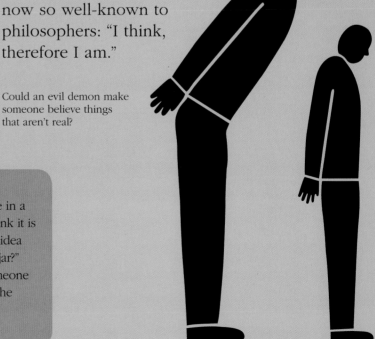

Brain in a jar
Suppose a person's brain has been removed and kept alive in a jar. It is linked to a computer and fed data that makes it think it is still in a body. A modern version of Descartes' evil demon idea asks "How do you know that you are not just a brain in a jar?" The answer is because you are wondering about it—if someone is controlling your brain, he or she would never give you the ability to think those thoughts in the first place.

René **Descartes**

"It is not enough to have a good mind; the main thing is to use it well."

Biography

1596 Born in La Haye en Touraine, France, a town later renamed Descartes in his honor. His mother dies when he is young, and he and his brother and sister are brought up by his grandmother.

1603–12 Educated at the College of La Flèche, Anjou, which is run by Jesuits (members of a Roman Catholic order). He studies mathematics, Classics, and philosophy, and comes to believe that math is the only subject worth studying.

1616 Graduates with a degree in law from the University of Poitiers, then enlists in military school.

1620–28 Travels around Europe. In 1625, he meets Father Marin Mersenne, a French philosopher and physicist, who encourages him to publish his scientific papers and introduces him to other philosophers.

1628 Settles in the Netherlands and begins writing his first work on physics.

1637 Publishes *Discourse on the Method*.

1640 Publishes *Meditations on First Philosophy*, arguing that the mind and body are different kinds of things.

1650 Dies of pneumonia at the age of 53 while working as a tutor at the Swedish royal court.

One of the world's most brilliant and original thinkers, Descartes is often called "the first modern philosopher." He broke away from the kind of thinking that the ancient Greeks had done and took a **new, scientific approach**. Descartes said that it was a mistake to try to gain knowledge about ourselves and the world by relying on our senses. He preferred to figure things out, like a mathematician faced with a tricky calculation.

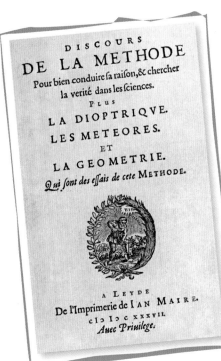

Discourse on the Method was published in 1637.

Famous works

Descartes began writing the books that made him famous in 1630. His early works were scientific, but in 1640 he published his best-known book, *Meditations on the First Philosophy*. In it he wrote about the mind and the differences between mind and body, and the book includes his famous words: "I think, therefore I am." What Descartes meant by this was that because he could think he could be absolutely sure he existed. He also wrote *Discourse on the Method*, one of the most influential philosophy books of all time.

Swedish downfall

Descartes steadily became more well-known. Queen Christina of Sweden was so impressed by his ideas that she invited him to come to Sweden to become her personal philosophy tutor. This turned out to be his downfall. Not only did he have to get up very early in the morning, which he had always disliked, but he also found Sweden unbearably cold. He became fatally ill and died less than a year after accepting the job.

Queen Christina of Sweden and members of her court listen as Descartes gives a philosophy lesson.

Influencing science

In addition to influencing generations of future philosophers, Descartes' writing also had an enormous impact on the scientific world. People such as the mathematician Isaac Newton and the astronomer Edmond Halley took great interest in Descartes' work on physics and mathematics. Descartes' work on the laws of motion led to Newton's own work on motion and, centuries later, made it possible to launch rockets into space.

Who am "I"?

Do you sometimes wonder which part of you is "you"?

When you say or think "I," do you mean your body? Or, like the philosopher René Descartes, do you mean your mind, the "thinking" part of you? Maybe you agree with Descartes that mind and body are two separate things. On the other hand, you might feel like a mixture of both. Could there be a correct answer?

Which part stays "me"?

You probably can't remember being a baby. Look at a picture of your younger self to see what you were once like. Your body is entirely different now. You can do things like walking, running, and jumping. Once you learned to speak you started thinking in a different way from a baby. Has any part of you stayed the same person?

As we grow up, we change a great deal in our body and mind.

Memories help us remember how to do things, such as ride a bike.

Am I my memories?

We have many different types of memories. Some help us remember how to do things, such as riding a bike or solving a math problem. Others remind us of events like a friend's birthday or what time a train arrives. Still others help us discover our likes and dislikes—for example, we remember if we enjoy the taste of chocolate. Perhaps putting all our memories together gives us a sense of who we are.

Fear

Disgust

Am I my feelings?

Memories often come with feelings attached to them. Do you remember the first time you met your best friend? Does the thought make you feel happy and want to smile? Feelings, or emotions, also help us decide what is the right or wrong thing to do. We don't all feel the same way about the same things. What makes one person want to dance with happiness may make another want to cry. Perhaps it is our feelings that make us who we are?

Does the way you feel about things make you the person you are?

Nonstop mind

The things in your mind—memories, emotions, likes, and dislikes—continue from day to day. Maybe it is the way they continue overlapping and linking together that makes you definitely "you"? But what if one stops? Suppose a man forgets everything that has ever happened to him and everyone he knows. But if he loves peanut butter and dancing as he used to, could we still say he is the same person?

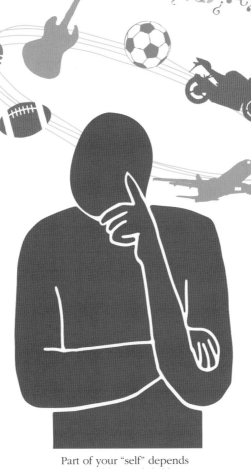

Part of your "self" depends on your likes and dislikes.

What is the self?

Am I just a machine?

Materialists are philosophers who think that everything about us is made of some kind of material. They say that even the mind is just a collection of thought-carrying brain cells firing away. This makes us sound like machines, but are we? Could a machine have feelings or worry about something?

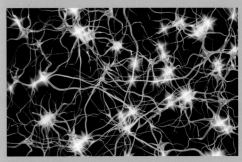

This magnified picture of brain cells shows how they link up to carry thoughts.

What came first?

Aristotle said that the most important part of anything is what he called its "final cause." This means the main reason for something to exist. So a fruit bowl's final cause is to hold fruit, for instance. A person's final cause is to be that particular person, or soul. Aristotle says the soul, which is real, comes first and creates the need for a body.

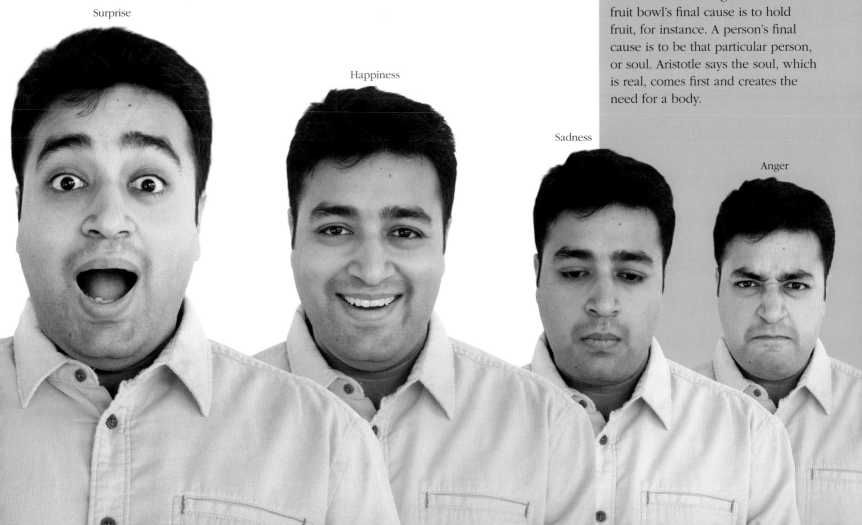

Surprise

Happiness

Sadness

Anger

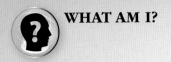

The life of Avicenna

980 Born near Bukhara in Central Asia, which is controlled by Persian rulers called the Samanids. His father was a village governor.

996 At the age of 16, he begins work as a doctor. He cures the Samanid ruler, Nuh Ibn Mansur, of an illness and is allowed to use the ruler's library as a reward.

999 When the Samanids are overthrown in Bukhara, he begins traveling. He works as a doctor and philosopher in royal courts, towns, and villages throughout Asia.

1025 Avicenna completes his *Canon of Medicine*, a collection of all his medical knowledge.

Avicenna's *Canon of Medicine*

1037 Dies in Hamadan, Persia.

The **Flying Man**

Known as Avicenna in the Western world, the Arabic physician Ibn Sina was one of the **most important medieval philosophers**. He wanted to know "Do I exist?" centuries before other thinkers asked the same question. In 1002, Avicenna used his "Flying Man" experiment to show that our minds are separate from our bodies.

To do Avicenna's experiment, we have to imagine a perfectly ordinary person who is normal in every way. However, this person has been blindfolded and is floating in the air. None of his arms or legs touch anything. He can't see, feel, smell, or taste. There is no noise, so he can't hear anything either. How does this Flying Man still know that he exists? Avicenna says that the man will know because he is thinking. But what exactly is the mind—or "self,"

as Avicenna calls it—that the Flying Man is using to think? He can't feel it in his head, and his sight, hearing, and other senses aren't picking up information from outside his body and sending it to his brain. Yet he is still able to have thoughts. So the experiment is a way of showing that the mind must be very different from the body. It can exist and think without help from the senses.

1	**Common sense**
2	**Imagination**
3	**Ideas**
4	**Thoughts**
5	**Memories**

Mind powers

Avicenna said that the mind has five powers, or inner senses. The first four are common sense, imagination, the ability to use ideas to create things, and the power to figure out what the thoughts and images in our heads mean. Finally, the mind is able to store as memories the things that pass through it. All these mind-powers let us pick up and make use of the information we receive through our body senses. This is how we keep ourselves safe, for instance—at least most of the time.

Even without his senses, the Flying Man can still think.

Think about it!

Mind and body are one

Avicenna believed that the mind was best imagined as being like a person operating a piece of equipment, which is the body. However, other philosophers say this isn't a good way to explain things. For example, if you hurt your arm, you notice the pain differently from the way a mechanic notices a fault in his machinery. Pain is something you feel instantly. The unpleasant sensation is part of "you," just as much as your thoughts about the cause of it belong to you. Your body is "you" too, not just a machine operated by your mind.

No ghosts in the body

Not everyone approved of the way Avicenna made the mind seem so mysterious. As one modern philosopher put it: the mind is just the workings of brain cells and nerves. We don't need to make it sound like some kind of strange ghost floating around inside the body. It's simpler to imagine that the mind is similar to a big school. The school is made up of classrooms, a library, a gym, a science laboratory, and so on. There's no one place you can point to and say "that's the school." The mind is lots of different things, too. Like the rooms in the school, these work together as part of something bigger. You can't point to one part and say "there's the mind."

Using imagination

According to Avicenna, our imagination has two parts. The first part is what goes on in our heads when we notice something that interests us. Our minds take in the details and start to wonder about them. The second part to the imagination is a skill that lets us change these mind-pictures and thoughts. We might mix them all together or turn them into completely different ones.

We can use the power of imagination to create works of art.

Is my mind different from my body?

Our minds and bodies mostly seem to get along fine. So do we really need to wonder **how they work together**? For centuries, philosophers have been doing just that. They have come up with a lot of different ideas. Some said the mind was solid like the body. Others said they were two different kinds of things. A few believed that only thoughts could exist.

Body and soul
The ancient Greek philosophers had lots of discussions about the soul, or mind. Some of them thought that body and soul were separate and when a person died the soul was set free to live forever. Others believed that body and soul were joined in some way. They said that the soul was made of solid matter and would die when the body died.

Split in two
After a lot of thinking and debating, philosopher René Descartes (1596–1650) came to the conclusion that body and mind are very different kinds of things. The body is made of matter, but the mind isn't. This view is called Dualism, and it is about dividing something into two parts. It led to some very big questions: how can the mind make parts of the body move? How can things felt by the body be understood by the mind?

God in charge
In the 11th-century, the Iranian philosopher al-Ghazali (c.1058–1111) decided that God must be in control of our thoughts and actions. He couldn't find any other explanation for the way thoughts and the body could work together. It seemed obvious that messages pass between the mind and body: for example, the mind tells the body to move, and the body tells the mind that a toe hurts. But how is this possible? Al-Ghazali believed that it had to be God who makes us think about moving an arm, and then makes the arm move.

Many philosophers have tried to figure out how the mind and the body work together.

Thomas Hobbes (1588–1679)

No difference

One group of philosophers believed that thoughts are made of types of matter, just like the body is made of matter. These philosophers are known as Materialists. Thomas Hobbes was a key Materialist thinker. He said that when things happen to the body, lots of little events occur in the body, one after another, like dominoes knocking each other over. So when a bee stings you, the skin reacts, sending a message to the brain, and ending with the thought "Ow!" If this idea is right, it suggests we aren't able to control our natural reactions.

Both sides of a coin

Another philosophical view is that mind and body are like two sides of a coin. When something happens to one, something also happens to the other. Imagine that a football hits you on the head. Your body hurts and at the same time your mind thinks "A football hit me!" Baruch Spinoza, the 17th-century philosopher who suggested the coin idea, believed that our actions and feelings are connected to nature, while our thoughts are connected to God.

Side by side

German philosopher Gottfried Wilhelm von Leibniz (1646–1716) said that our minds and bodies are not linked. If the body wants to do the same things as the mind, it is because God planned it. Von Leibniz thought that the universe had two paths running side by side. On one path are things that can be seen and touched, such as the body. On the other path are things concerning the mind. Like two clocks ticking next to one another, these paths run on at the same time, but never cross over.

What body?

Have you ever thought that perhaps your body isn't there at all? Irish philosopher Bishop Berkeley (1685–1753) did. In fact, he doubted that there was anything solid in the world. As far as he was concerned, only the mind and its thoughts really exist. He believed that the body, and any other things we consider real, are nothing more than ideas in the mind.

Body or brain?

The shoemaker-prince

As long ago as 1689, John Locke tried to figure out whether it is the brain or the body that makes us who we are. He imagined the mind of a prince being transplanted into the body of a shoemaker. The prince's mind was unchanged, so the shoemaker had the thoughts, memories, and personality of the prince. However, the prince's mind was in the shoemaker's body, so the combined person wasn't the same as the prince. How could he be both the same and yet not the same?

The body counts, too

American philosopher Eric Olson says that the body is just as important as the brain when it comes to determining what makes people who they are. He points out that a body has lived in the same places and experienced the same things as the mind, so they share a history. The body also has a nervous system that tells every part of it, including the brain, what to do. So, Eric Olson reasons, our bodies count as "us."

This famous sculpture is called *The Thinker.*

Shoemaker's
brain experiment

Philosophers have puzzled for a long time about the connection between the mind and the body. The mind is not a thing like an arm, so how does it get in touch with the body to tell it what to do? More importantly, **which part of me is "me"?** Do my friends know who I am because of my body or because of my mind? The philosopher Sydney Shoemaker came up with a thought experiment to look at this in more detail.

Is it what goes on in people's brains that makes them who they are? After all, the mind makes all the decisions that guide us through life and seems to be in charge of everything that we do. In fact, most people agree that our minds are more the real "us" than our bodies. Sydney Shoemaker thought that things might not be quite as simple as that. He wanted to make us think more carefully about the way minds and bodies go together, so he devised a thought experiment. He came up with the following story:

Two people, Jack and Tom, have brain surgery. Their brains are taken out of their bodies to be operated on. The brains are then replaced, but something goes wrong—they are put back into the wrong bodies. Jack's body ends up with Tom's brain, and Tom's body gets Jack's brain. Then, sadly, Jack dies, with Tom's brain still inside him. Tom (with Jack's brain) recovers. The question is: who is this surviving person?

When friends pay a visit to the survivor, they at first think of him as Tom, because he looks like Tom. But the more they speak to him, the more confused they get. He seems to like and want the things Jack wanted. He appears to love soccer and says he wants to go and see his team playing in Argentina. But before the brain mix-up Tom wasn't interested in sports and disliked traveling. He also remembers the things that have happened in Jack's life. What's more, this person wants to go home to Jack's wife and children. So who is he? Tom or Jack?

If one person swapped minds with another, which person would be which? Both would look the same as before, but they would each speak and behave as if they were the other person.

Think about it!

Moveable minds

The problem of "who's who?" gets even more complicated if we imagine that more than just two people are involved in a mind-replacement experiment. Perhaps in the future it will be possible to wipe thoughts from brains, like deleting data from a computer disk, and input different thoughts. Suppose we took a person's mind—with all its memories, likes and dislikes, and so on—and copied it into blank brains in lots of other bodies. What would we think about these people who now possess identical minds? Are they really all the same or would we see each one as different?

Why is the brain so important?

If we think it's the brain that makes a person who they are, even supposing it was placed in a different body, why isn't it the same with other organs? For instance, if a woman has a heart transplant, would we ever say that the real survivor is the one who donated her heart? The brain seems to be a special case. It is the organ that allows us to think in a continuous way from day to day. We can pick up our thoughts this morning from where we left them last night. Mostly, our beliefs and wishes stay the same.

Memory loss

There is yet another problem with saying that our continuing thoughts make us who we are. Sometimes people's minds stop being able to pass on thoughts from one day to the next. This is a medical condition called amnesia, when people lose all their memories. If someone can't remember anything, are they still the same person?

How do we learn?

Philosophers are very interested in knowledge, especially in **what we know and how we know it**. There is a big philosophical debate about whether we learn things by thinking about them or by experiencing them. One group of philosophers suggests that we are born with some ideas already in our heads. Others disagree completely.

Born with ideas

René Descartes suggested that some of our ideas exist in our minds even before we are born. He said that we might not be aware of having these ideas, but they are like rules that we use to make sense of the world. They include mathematical ideas such as shapes and sizes. Without these ideas, Descartes said, the world would seem like a big, colorful, energetic mess that made no sense at all.

Working it out

One of the ideas that Descartes said we are born with is "cause and effect." For example, when a baby hits a mobile and it moves, what makes him hit it again? Descartes would say it is because the baby already understands the idea of cause and effect, so he knows that the force of his hand will make the mobile move. But John Locke said this was wrong. He said that a baby has no ideas, but is able to work things out. So he would say that the baby just happens to hit the mobile again, and again, and starts to notice that the hand and mobile movement seem connected.

Babies learn very early on in their lives that hitting a mobile makes it move.

No set ideas

Locke said that if people were born with ideas already in their minds then every human being everywhere in the world, at any time throughout history, would have exactly the same ideas. But no one has ever found an idea that exists everywhere in this way. This seems to confirm Locke's suggestion that we are not born with set ideas already in our heads, but instead have to learn everything for ourselves as we grow up.

Locke said it is impossible for everyone in the world to share the same idea.

Hidden ideas

To support his argument that all our ideas are learned through experience, Locke reasoned that if we were born with ideas already in our heads then we would know about them. Because we don't know about these ideas, then they can't be there. However, other philosophers say that Locke could be wrong about this. They argue that we don't know every single one of our memories, until we try to remember them. For example, you might have forgotten what you did last weekend, until someone asks you about it. Perhaps the ideas we are born with are just like our memories—in our minds, just waiting to be found?

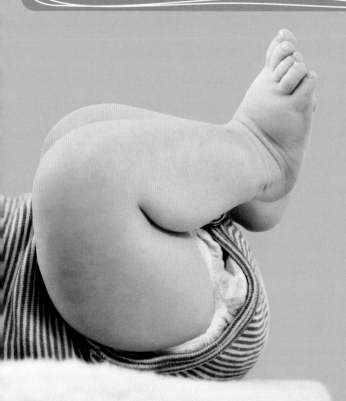

An "apple" is a bundle of simple ideas—it is round, red, sweet, and juicy.

Making links

Scottish philosopher David Hume (1711–76) said that we learn by linking things together. He said that we use the information we get through our senses—what we see, hear, feel, smell, and taste—to make simple ideas, such as the color "red." Then we link our simple ideas together to make more complex ideas, for instance, "apple."

Biography

1632 Born in Somerset, England.

1642 Locke's father fights in the English Civil War against King Charles I.

1652 Goes to Christ Church College, Oxford University, where he stays for 30 years.

1666 Works as a doctor for Lord Ashley, who later became the Earl of Shaftesbury, also helping him with business and political matters.

1683 Flees to the Netherlands after he is suspected of helping to plan a rebellion.

1688 Returns to England.

1689 Takes up a job in the English government, anonymously publishes *Two Treatises of Government*, outlining his ideas of natural law.

1690 Publishes *An Essay Concerning Human Understanding*.

1696 Becomes the Commissioner of Trade and Plantations.

1691 Moves to Oates in Essex.

1704 Dies at age 72.

John Locke

"Where there is no law, there is no freedom."

John Locke was one of the most important thinkers of the 17th century. This was a time when people were beginning to trust tradition less and wanted to figure things out for themselves—it was known as the Age of Enlightenment. Locke was an important politician as well as a philosopher. His **ideas about power influenced people** in many countries, including the newly formed United States.

Early years

John Locke's father was a lawyer who fought for the Parliamentarians in the English Civil War. His side won, and to thank the Locke family, the Parliamentarians paid for John Locke to study at Oxford University. He stayed there for 30 years, studying philosophy and medicine, and then worked for 10 years as a doctor.

Christ Church College, Oxford

Natural law

Locke believed that people have the right to control their own bodies, and no one should tell them what to do with them. He also said that when a person works on something, it becomes theirs—for example, if you were to make a gate from pieces of wood, you would own the gate. Locke called his ideas "natural law," and wrote about them in *Two Treatises of Government*. These ideas went on to influence generations around the world.

The United States Declaration of Independence includes Locke's idea of natural law. It was signed in 1776.

Experiencing the world

Locke thought that people are not born with knowledge of the world, but have to experience the world to learn about it. He said that objects have two types of qualities—primary qualities, such as shape and size, which are in the thing itself, and secondary qualities, such as color and smell, which occur in our minds when we experience an object.

Locke says that the colors of these flowers are in our minds, rather than in the flowers themselves.

53

How *do* **I** *know* *what* **you're** *thinking?*

How can we prove that other people have minds that work in the same way as our own? Each of us has unique access to his or her own mind— no one can read another person's mind. But if **we don't know how someone else's mind works**, how do we know what that person is thinking?

We assume these children are happy because they look the way we feel when we are happy.

Other minds

We can't get inside another person's mind to see what it is like, but we can see how others behave. John Locke said that watching other people's behavior leads us to assume their minds are like our own. However, these observations don't give us actual knowledge, since they are based on our own ideas, which are still only in our own heads!

Why do you think this person is frowning?

Understanding behavior

Imagine that you see someone walk up to a store, find it closed, frown, and walk away. Based on your own experience, you might assume that the person felt frustrated. However, that person's mind and body might operate very differently from yours. Perhaps that person frowns when thinking hard, and therefore may not be annoyed at all.

We use language to show our feelings.

The language game

Austrian philosopher Ludwig Wittgenstein said that we have developed language to help us share our experiences with other people. Language lets us make our private thoughts public, and we can only talk if we understand what is being said. So language proves that there are other minds, because it represents shared thoughts—things that lots of us think or feel. Without language we wouldn't know that we think and feel in similar ways.

Feelings are common

If there is a word for something, it means that many people have experienced it. For example, if you start using the word "pain" in the wrong way, you will soon realize you are wrong by the way other people react to you. From a young age, you learn to use the word to describe the same kinds of feelings that others do. Learning language lets you learn about feelings that everyone has. If you use a new word to describe something that only you have ever felt, no one will correct you. They just won't know what you're talking about!

Language and feelings

Is my pain the same as your pain?

Even if you explain to your best friend exactly what happens when you stub your toe, can he or she really know what it is like to experience that in your body and mind? It's possible that if you asked 10 other people to describe the feeling of stubbing their toe, they would all use the word "pain," but they could all be feeling it differently. How can we know exactly what they are feeling?

Stubbing your toe is painful, but do we all feel the pain in the same way?

Similar experiences

We all think we experience the same feelings. But how do we know we all feel the same thing when we say we are happy, hungry, excited, or tired? Wittgenstein would say that this does not really matter— our experiences are similar enough. We can understand enough about what is happening to those people, even if we cannot experience their actual feelings.

Biography

c.563 BCE Born under a tree when his mother is on a journey. It is said that he took seven steps as soon as he was born, and a lotus flower sprung up at every step.

The young Buddha and his mother

c.547 BCE Gets married at the age of 16. Some time after this he leaves his home, the palace, for the first time.

c.547–483 BCE Travels, visiting wise people and trying to find a solution to human suffering. Eventually he reaches enlightenment, under a tree. He becomes known as the Buddha and spends the rest of his life traveling and teaching.

c.483 BCE Dies at the age of 80.

Siddhartha Gautama

"There is no law that is permanent and unchangeable."

Siddhartha Gautama became known as the Buddha, or "the enlightened one." His teachings form the core of Buddhism, an Eastern philosophy. Buddhism is based on the idea that **nothing in the world is permanent**. The Buddha said that human suffering is caused by people trying to keep things as they are in a world of constant change.

Early life

Brought up in a royal court, Siddhartha Gautama didn't know what life was like outside the palace gates. As a young man he was shocked to discover the existence of illness, old age, and death. He left his princely life and vowed to find the answer to human suffering. To try and do this he traveled widely, learning from religious teachers, but eventually he realized that they didn't know the answer. He then sat down under a tree to think and to try and find the answers in himself.

Siddhartha Gautama was saddened to discover human suffering outside his palace home.

The Buddha

Siddhartha Gautama stayed under his tree for 49 days. Sitting under the tree, he thought about what was important in life and how people should live. His conclusion was that even though sickness, old age, and death would always exist, we can change our reaction to them. This moment of realization is known as his "enlightenment," and from this point onward Siddhartha Gautama was known as the Buddha.

Statue of the Buddha

The Middle Way

One of the Buddha's main ideas is known as the Middle Way. It says that truth cannot be found in the unbending beliefs of religions or in doubting everything, but somewhere in between the two. The Buddha said that we should not just accept things the way other people say they are, but investigate everything with our own minds. We should become aware of our thoughts, which arise and disappear, like everything else in a world that is constantly changing.

The Wheel of Law represents change and the endless cycle of life.

Finding happiness

The Buddha said that the truth of the world is that everything changes. Nothing is permanent—things arise and then disappear, including ourselves. But even though we can't stop things from changing, we keep wanting things to stay the same. For example, you might want a party to last forever and get upset about the idea that it must end. Buddhism said that it is this "wanting" that is upsetting you, before the party even ends. Enjoy the party, and if you feel sad when it ends, just allow yourself to feel the sadness, because that will end quickly too.

What *is the* "self"?

Philosophers have spent thousands of years questioning **what we mean by the "self."** How do we know a person is that particular person? Is a person the same as a baby and as an adult? Buddhism says we shouldn't worry about these kinds of questions. This is because there is another, much bigger question to answer before all the rest: is there such a thing as the self in the first place?

Everything changes

According to the Buddha, if there were such a thing as a self it would have to stay the same over our whole lives, never changing in any way. But when we look at ourselves, we can see that we are changing all the time. It's not just our bodies that alter. We change our minds about things and our thoughts can be different from one day to the next. The Buddha said that we call ourselves "I" only because it makes it easier to talk to each other and to conduct our lives.

What is "me"?

Some philosophers see the mind and body as different types of things. They wonder whether the mind, or soul, lives on when we die. Others say that the mind is just the workings of the brain. So when we die and the brain stops working, the mind stops, too. Both groups agree that there is a soul, or "me," in a body. But Buddhists believe there is no such thing as a soul. They think "me" is an illusion, a mistaken idea.

Buddhists believe that we are ever-changing, just like trees.

We can think of ourselves as a collection of different parts, in much the same way as this watch.

Explaining the self

This story is about a monk, Nagasena, explaining the idea of the self. He tells a king that there is no such person as Nagasena. This surprises the king—he says that Nagasena is a name, and names are used only when they belong to something. If "Nagasena" is not a name, it means nothing. So the monk asks the king to explain what a chariot is. The king names parts of a chariot, such as the wheels and seat. Nagasena says yes, those are the parts—but where is the chariot? The king realizes that there isn't anything called a chariot that is separate from the parts. But, he says, it is useful that we all know what is meant by "chariot." Exactly, says Nagasena. That is also true of the self.

Can we say what a chariot is without thinking of its different parts?

Nothing but parts

Many philosophers believe that each individual, or self, is made up of all the parts of the mind and body added together. This would include our feelings, wishes, and thoughts. On the other hand, Buddhism says that if you break down the "self" into all those different parts, that's all there is—parts. The parts may be there, but there is no whole "me." If we take away the parts, then there is nothing left.

Plutarch

The ancient Greek historian and philosopher Plutarch wrote about history and the famous people who made history, such as Alexander the Great and Julius Caesar. He was also interested in identity, morals—good and bad ways to act—and how people's characters affected their futures.

Plutarch at his studies.

46 Born in the village of Chaeronea, Greece, to a wealthy family.

66–67 Studies math and philosophy at Plato's The Academy in Athens.

c.70–75 Travels around Greece and to Sparta, Alexandria, and Rome, where he becomes a Roman citizen, with the new name of Lucius Mestrius Plutarchus. Marries Timoxena, with whom he has at least one daughter and four sons.

c.75 Returns to Chaeronea, where he becomes the senior priest at the Oracle of Delphi, making predictions about people's futures.

c.96 Publishes his first famous book, *The Lives of the Roman Emperors*.

c.120 Dies in Delphi, Greece.

The ship *of* Theseus

How many parts can you take away from a thing and still say that it is the same thing? Plutarch investigated this question using the story of an ancient ship that once belonged to Theseus, an ancient Greek hero who founded the city of Athens. His story poses a problem that has fascinated philosophers for centuries.

Theseus was a great hero to the people of Athens. When he returned home after a war, the ship that had carried him and his men was so treasured that the townspeople preserved it for years and years, replacing its old, rotten planks with new pieces of wood. The question Plutarch asks philosophers is this: is the repaired ship still the same ship that Theseus had sailed? Removing one plank and replacing it might not make a difference, but can that still be true once all the planks have been replaced?

Some philosophers argue that the ship must be the sum of all its parts. But if this is true, then as the ship got pushed around during its journey and lost small pieces, it would already have stopped being the ship of Theseus.

Others argue that the ship is the ship of Theseus because of its structure, or shape. But if this is the case, any ship that was the same structure or shape would be the ship of Theseus, even if it were made of plastic. That would mean that there could be hundreds or thousands of the same ship, all of which are the ship of Theseus—but this is impossible, since he only sailed in one ship.

What is it that makes us able to point to something and say exactly what it is?

Would a ship still be the same ship after all its original parts had been replaced with new ones?

Two ships or no ships?

If the old planks that have been removed from Theseus's ship were used to build another ship, would that ship be the ship of Theseus? The two ships can't both be the ship of Theseus. It might be true that neither of them is. In that case, when was the ship of Theseus destroyed?

Would a second ship made from the pieces of the old one be the real ship of Theseus?

Think about it!

Personal identity

The story about Theseus's ship is about identity—what makes a thing what it is? We can think about people in the same way. For example, we think of ourselves as being the same person we always were, even though our bodies make new cells and blood all the time. Our skin cells are replaced every seven days, and all our body cells every seven years. That's like replacing all the planks of Theseus's ship over and over again. Are we still the same person? And if so, in what way?

Identical people

Just as we could make an exact replica of Theseus's ship, future scientists may be able to clone humans, making a new person who is identical to someone else. It is possible that they could even put all the same memories into the new, cloned person. Who is the second person, if the two people are completely identical?

What about consciousness?

Some philosophers have argued that people are different from ships. A person is more than just physical skin and cells—he or she has ideas, thoughts, and memories. But what is it, exactly, that makes us feel so sure that someone is the same person over time? What makes Sarah, age 8, the same person as Sarah, age 98?

Is there life after death?

We are the only animals who are aware that one day we will die. But philosophers say that all we really know is that one day our bodies will stop working. **Could there be a part of us that goes on after death?** This question has fascinated people for thousands of years. Could philosophers ever prove what really happens?

Epicurus said that the mind can't live without the body.

Do souls live forever?

Some philosophers said that only ideas are real. They also decided that real things last forever. So, if "I" am my thoughts, and thoughts are ideas, I am real and will last forever. My body is not an "idea," so it will die. Some cultures and religions believe that when someone dies we can contact the "idea" part of them, which lives on.

Nothing lasts

A lot of people believe that the mind is part of the body and can't go on living once the body dies. The ancient Greek philosopher Epicurus pointed out that this idea is very comforting—it means that we won't be around to know what death is like.

It is the custom in some religions to make offerings to spirits. These people in China are burning candles, incense sticks, and paper money for relatives who have died.

Everlasting mind

Some philosophers say that the mind and body are made of completely different things. They see the body as a machine that will eventually stop working and die. But because the mind is not made of anything solid, they believe that it might be everlasting. The problem these philosophers have is that they can't explain how mind (thoughts) and body (a physical thing) join together. This link is important. Our minds and bodies might be very different, but can one exist without the other?

Could our minds live on after our bodies?

Living many lives

In ancient times, many people believed in reincarnation. This is the idea that the soul lives on after death and is reborn into a new body. Among those who accepted such an idea were the Greeks, Egyptians, Celts, Scandinavians, American Indians, Chinese, and many African tribes. The Greeks believed that when people died they went to the underworld, which was called Hades. Then people were reborn over and over again. After many lives, they eventually became good enough to go and stay with the gods forever.

The soul in the afterlife

Several of the world's major religions state that when people die their souls live on in an afterlife. There are various ideas about what this will be like. Many religions include the belief that their God will judge how well the person behaved in the world before letting the soul move on to a better life.

Going to heaven

Christians believe that their souls go to heaven when they die. Some see heaven as a real place. Others say that heaven is not a place, but instead is a way of being together with God. Muslims also believe that the soul enters heaven, where there is everlasting peace and happiness.

Being with Brahman

Followers of Hinduism believe in reincarnation—they think that they will be reborn after death. Hindus hope that their souls will eventually be freed from the cycle of rebirth by good deeds. Then they can join Brahman, who, together with Vishnu and Shiva, is one of the three most important Hindu gods.

The Hindu god Shiva is associated with the cycle of death and reincarnation.

Thinking *and* feeling

Our minds are busy working all the time.
We have to think to solve problems and make decisions, and we use language to share ideas. We also have feelings, hopes, and dreams.

Can we **think without language?**

Before they can use language, babies can't reason—
they think in terms of images and sensations.

Among animals, humans have the unique ability to use spoken and written language. Language helps us express complicated ideas and allows us to think about more than simply what we can experience with our senses. **Perhaps it is because we can use language that we are able to think in the way we do**.

Uses of language

Whether it is spoken or written, language lets us communicate ideas to other people. We can discuss things, agree or disagree with other people's ideas, and come up with new ideas of our own. We use language to communicate with ourselves, too—having a kind of "inner conversation" where we discuss ideas with ourselves in our minds.

Thinking and reasoning

The word "think" means many different things. But there is a difference between having a thought or feeling, and using reasoning—thinking about something rationally. For example, we can think that something tastes good, but that is not the same as thinking through a problem. This kind of rational thought is almost impossible without some form of language.

Using language, a teacher can explain complicated ideas to her students, and they can ask her questions.

Thinking in pictures

There are some things that we can think about without using language. For example, when we imagine a machine and how it works, we usually think visually, in pictures. Pictures are often more useful than language to think about things we can see or touch. But pictures cannot communicate abstract ideas such as goodness or fairness. It is difficult to express a complex idea, such as "Jim won't come if it is raining," in a picture. To think about these more complex things, we need language.

A silent movie can deliver a simple plot, and even express the emotions of the characters, but it cannot tell a complicated story.

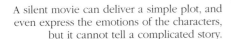

Some mythical creatures, such as the unicorn, came from descriptions of exotic animals that travelers had come across but that they didn't have words for.

How do deaf people think?
People who have been deaf from birth learn language differently than people who can hear. They cannot easily learn spoken language, but can learn sign language, and to read and write. Deaf people may not have the sounds of words in their heads when they have a conversation, or even an internal conversation, but they do use a language. They use this soundless form of language to reason, just as hearing people use spoken language.

Limits of language

Without language, our thinking would be restricted to the things we experience through our senses. Language allows us to use our reasoning. But there are things that we cannot express with language—things we haven't experienced and we don't have words for. It is difficult to think about things we have no language for. People living in a desert, for example, might not have a word for "snow" in their language. Without a word for it, they would find it difficult to express the idea of snow if they came across it.

Understanding languages

Learning language
Most of the time, we use language without thinking about it. It seems to come naturally, and at a very early age. Philosopher and psychologist Noam Chomsky (1928–) says that humans are born with a unique natural ability to learn language. He has pointed out that a kitten exposed to exactly the same language and environment as a baby would never pick up language in the way the baby would—learning language is uniquely human.

Learning spoken language is something that only humans seem able to do.

Do animals use language?
Animals are not able to use words like humans. They do, however, have ways of communicating with each other, using sounds and signs to communicate ideas such as "danger" or "food." Some people say that this type of communication is not really language, since it cannot be used to express complicated ideas.

Chimps use signs and sounds to communicate with each other.

Reasoning *and* arguments

When philosophers present an idea, or theory, they try to explain why they think it is true. They arrive at their idea by thinking around a question or a problem and then **present their thoughts in a logical way**. Philosophers show the steps they take from what they already know to the conclusion—their new idea. The rules of logic help us to decide whether or not we are convinced by an argument.

This 13th century manuscript shows Socrates debating with his pupils.

Talking it through

The Greek philosopher Socrates spent his time talking with other people. He asked them questions—such as "What is justice?"—as if he knew nothing about the subject. Then he examined their answers, pointing out when they didn't make sense, and asked more questions. By reasoning in this way, he showed if an argument was strong or weak.

Figuring it out

One form of logical argument is made up from three statements. The first two statements are things that we know for certain. From them we can figure out the third statement, which is the conclusion. For example, we know that all cats are animals. And all lions are cats. So we can come to the conclusion that all lions are animals. When the conclusion follows on from the first two statements like this, the argument is said to be valid.

ANIMALS

CATS

LIONS

It must be true

Some arguments start from a general rule—for instance, "all monkeys eat bananas"—and a particular case, for example, "Mickey is a monkey." We can figure out from the general rule and particular case the conclusion that "Mickey eats bananas." This is an example of a "deductive" argument. If the general rule and the particular case at the beginning of such an argument are true, then the conclusion must also be true.

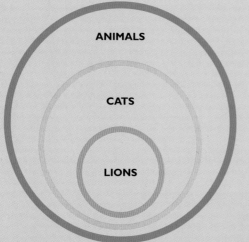

Probability

Not all logical arguments lead to a definite conclusion. Some only show whether something is likely to be true. Many arguments contain words such as "some" or "most," rather than "all." For example, we know that most tennis players are right-handed, and that Ann plays tennis, so it is probable that Ann is right-handed. This statement is not, however, necessarily true.

Exceptions to the rule

When we come up with a general rule based on individual cases, we are using "inductive" reasoning. For example, we see many individual cats. Every cat we see has a tail. But that does not necessarily mean that all cats have tails—there may be a cat somewhere without a tail. The next cat we see is very likely to have a tail, but we cannot say for certain that it will.

The problem with conclusions

Scientists use reasoning to develop theories. They observe and experiment, and if they see the same thing again and again, they say that there is a general rule. After seeing hundreds of white swans, scientists may conclude that all swans are white. But this only a theory—it is not necessarily true. You can show that "all swans are white" is false by finding just one black swan. Austrian philosopher Karl Popper (1902–94) said that for any theory to be scientific, there must be a way to show that it might be false. If it is impossible to show that a theory is false then it is not scientific.

Two kinds of truth

Philosophers use logical arguments to try to show if something is true or not. But Scottish philosopher David Hume (1711–76) and German philosopher Gottfried Leibniz (1646–1716) both argued that there is more than one kind of truth. We can see that some things are true just by thinking about them. For example, that an equilateral triangle has three equal sides and three equal angles. But there are also things that we can only know are true if we check the facts, such as "James lives in New York."

Do we think like computers?

Modern technology has allowed us to make machines and computers that can do almost everything that we can—sometimes better and quicker than us. It often seems like machines can think, and even have personalities. But we know that machines do not think like us. **What is it that makes our thinking different from the way machines work?** Perhaps we have something—a mind or a soul—that machines can never have.

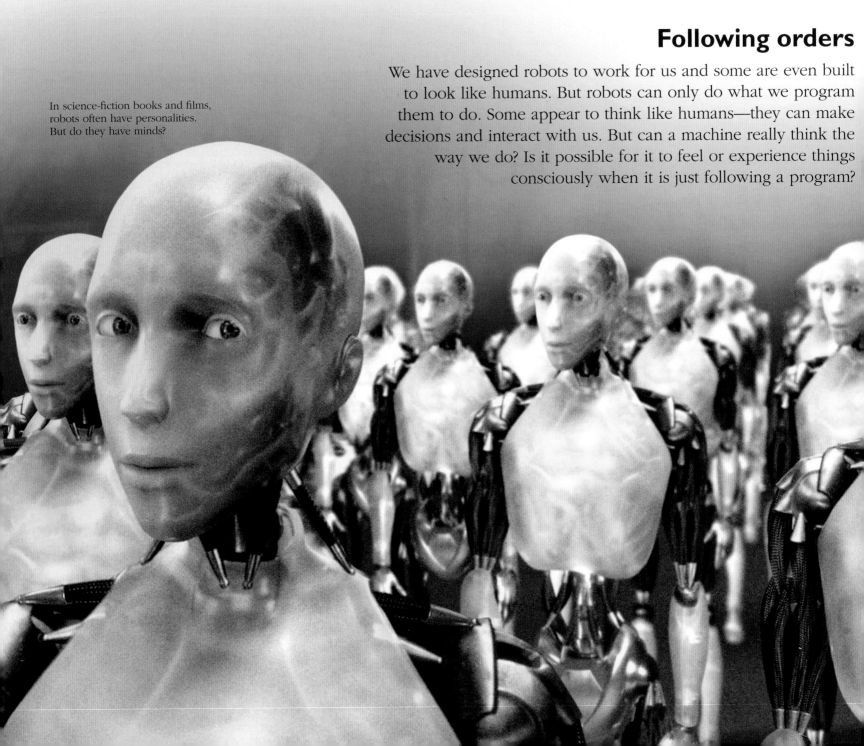

In science-fiction books and films, robots often have personalities. But do they have minds?

Following orders

We have designed robots to work for us and some are even built to look like humans. But robots can only do what we program them to do. Some appear to think like humans—they can make decisions and interact with us. But can a machine really think the way we do? Is it possible for it to feel or experience things consciously when it is just following a program?

Philosophical zombies

Philosophers like to talk about zombies. However, they mean something very different from the zombies in horror movies. Philosophical zombies look and behave just like normal people. If you hurt them, they shout "Ouch!" But they don't feel anything because they don't have minds. Robots and machines can be thought of as philosophical zombies—however clever they are, they don't possess emotions and feelings in the way that people do.

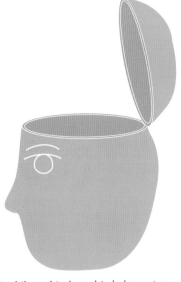

A philosophical zombie behaves just as we do, but has no feelings.

The ghost in the machine

Sometimes we are tricked into thinking that a computer can think for itself. Philosophers say this is like finding a "ghost in the machine"—a mind that just isn't there. However, some philosophers think that our brains are like very sophisticated computers. If computers don't have minds, how can we be sure that we do?

Computers can give the illusion that they have conscious minds. Do our brains create the same illusion?

Are animals like machines?

For a long time, philosophers thought that humans were different from animals because we have a soul or mind and they don't. René Descartes said that animals are not able to reason like we can. They have no minds or feelings—they are like machines that only appear to be conscious of what they are doing. But in the 19th century, Charles Darwin showed that humans are just a kind of animal, and people started to think that other animals might have feelings, too.

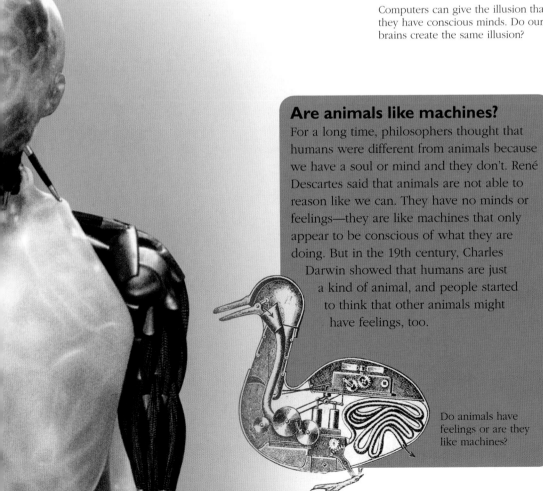

Do animals have feelings or are they like machines?

The rise of thinking machines

1822 Charles Babbage invents the first mechanical calculating machine, called a "difference engine."

Babbage's "difference engine"

1880s Herman Hollerith invents a method of storing data on punch cards that can be read by a machine—the first computer "memory."

1940s The first electronic digital programmable computer, Colossus, appears in the UK, followed by the ENIAC computer in the US—computers can now respond to questions and problems.

1960s Computers become smaller and more powerful with the invention of the integrated circuit or "microchip." These computers can solve many different kinds of problem, in a similar way to the human brain.

2014 Google releases Google Glass—computers are smaller and more portable than ever before.

Google Glass works from within our field of vision—perhaps one day computers will work as an extension of our minds.

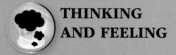
Thinking machines

The Turing test

Mathematician Alan Turing invented a test that shows whether a machine has real intelligence. A computer and a person are given the same set of written questions, and both must give written replies. Someone else then looks at the replies, and if it's impossible to tell which come from the computer and which from the person, the computer passes the test.

Alan Turing (1912–54) was a pioneer of computer science and artificial intelligence.

Artificial intelligence

Research into artificial intelligence (AI) developed in the 1950s, when people were learning just how powerful modern computers can be. The goal of scientists and engineers working in AI is to design "intelligent" machines that imitate the way people think. Some researchers believe that one day machines might be able to outthink the brainiest humans, but others doubt that this is possible.

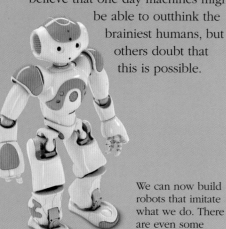

We can now build robots that imitate what we do. There are even some things that robots do better than us.

The Chinese room

Since the invention of computers, people have been asking "Can machines think?" American philosopher John Searle doesn't believe anyone can build a thinking machine. To show how we might be **fooled into believing a computer really is intelligent**, he used the "Chinese room" thought experiment. This is an example of how people, not only machines, may appear to understand something when they are just mindlessly obeying instructions.

Suppose, John Searle said, someone who can't speak a word of Chinese is put into a room on his own. He is given a set of cards with Chinese symbols written on them and a set of instructions in his own language telling him what to do. Then someone outside sends in more cards with Chinese symbols on them, which are questions that the man must answer. He turns to his instructions for help. These tell him which of his own cards he must send in reply to the different symbols. Of course, he has absolutely no idea what the written characters mean on either set of cards. To him they are just shapes and patterns. But the cards he sends out of the room turn out to be sensible replies to the questions. To anyone outside the room who speaks Chinese, it appears that the person inside understands the language perfectly and has had no trouble answering the questions. In fact, as we know, the person in the room can't understand Chinese symbols at all, so he wasn't able to read the questions or know what answers he had sent out. He simply followed the instructions.

This is exactly what happens with a computer. By the way a machine responds to data—the information it is given to process—it can make us believe that it knows what it is doing and seems to be thinking. But, like the person in the Chinese room, the machine is only following a set of instructions, a computer program written by someone with a real brain. Searle is showing us that thoughts and understanding involve a great deal more than processing data.

To someone in the "Chinese room," the symbols on these cards have no meaning. But the person doesn't need to know what the symbols say. As long as he has the right instructions he can respond to the cards correctly.

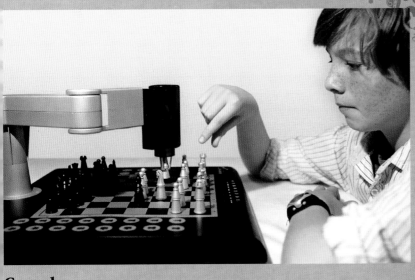

Today there are computer programs that can win games of chess against the world's best players.

Complex moves

Playing chess well requires skill and intelligence. The rules of the game are simple, but there are an almost endless number of possible moves. We can "teach" a computer to follow the rules and choose moves from its memory bank. Machines can even be programmed to plan several moves in advance. But many people believe that a computer could never learn to have the "feeling" for the game that truly great human chess players possess.

Think about it!

Can machines have feelings?

The Chinese room experiment shows how a machine that appears to be thinking is simply dealing with the data fed into it. In the same way, computers can be programmed so that they seem to have real feelings. For example, it is possible to make a machine shout "Ouch!" if you hit it, but, of course, it does not actually feel any pain.

Are our brains simply soft machines?

Computer science has helped us to understand the way we think. Our brains work like information processors and have been described as a kind of "soft machine." Computers can do some things, like complicated calculations, better and quicker than we can. Yet we still feel that our brains are more than just machines. Why should we think that? Is it because we are aware of having thoughts and feelings? Or because we are creative and come up with clever new ideas? Is it because we have a "mind" as well as a physical brain?

Can we ever make a machine that thinks like we do?

Even the smartest machines today are not aware of what they are doing or thinking. We have computers that can scan an image and recognize different faces—but they aren't really seeing in the way we do. Perhaps soon we will be able to make machines that can do almost everything people can. But they will probably never truly be "thinking machines." And how would we know for certain if they were?

Are words *like* signs?

Language is an important part of our everyday lives. We use it to communicate with each other and to think about things. Using words, we can express our thoughts and talk about objects and ideas. But **language is only useful if the words we use mean something to us**. What is it about the words we speak and write that gives them meaning?

balloon.

This girl connects the sound of the word "balloons" in her mind with the objects in her hand.

Words and meaning

When we talk or write about something, we use words. Each word means something to us. But many philosophers think that a word doesn't actually have a meaning. They say words are just a sound we make or marks on a page, but each word is like a sign that represents an object or idea— and when we hear or see the word, it makes us think of that object.

A system of signs

American philosopher C. S. Peirce (1839–1914) said that when we hear a word, we think of it as a sign representing an object. Swiss philosopher Ferdinand de Saussure (1857–1913) built on this idea with the suggestion that we keep the sound of a word in our minds. He said this sound represents an object or idea, and the meaning of a word connects the sound with its idea.

This street sign represents the same idea as the words "Do not enter."

Different words

Words for the same thing are often very different in different languages. When we see or hear a word, such as "dog," in our own language, we know what it means. We associate it in our minds with the animal. But to someone who does not know English, "dog" does not mean anything. And if we see the word "chien," it does not represent anything unless we know French. Words themselves have no meaning unless we recognize their connection with an object.

perro
dog
hund
chien
gou

To an English speaker this is a "dog," but it is a "chien" in French, "hund" in German, "gou" in Chinese, and "perro" in Spanish.

Picturing the world

Language helps us to understand the world around us. We use language to describe the things we experience and put everything together to build up a "picture" in our minds. But our mental picture of the world is limited by the things we can describe through language. There may be more to the world than the words we have to describe things and experiences.

We can describe this scene using words. But the picture in our minds could never be as accurate as seeing a photograph or the real thing.

Language and philosophy

Philosophy deals with reasoning—thinking about ideas. Because we express our thoughts and ideas in words, many philosophers have taken an interest in how language works—what words actually mean.

Logic and language

Language is especially important in logic, since philosophical ideas and arguments are mostly expressed in words. Philosophers such as Englishman Bertrand Russell (1872–1970) and Austrian Ludwig Wittgenstein (1889–1951) said that to judge whether an argument is good or not, we need to analyze its language carefully to uncover its meaning.

Philosophy of language

Some philosophers are interested in language itself, instead of language just as a way of communicating ideas. Philosophers C. S. Peirce and Ferdinand de Saussure developed theories about the meaning of words and how we interpret them that opened up a new field—the philosophy of language.

Philosopher Ferdinand de Saussure

Biography

1889 Born in Vienna, Austria.

1908 Travels to Manchester, UK, to study engineering.

1911 Becomes interested in logic and moves to Cambridge, UK.

1918 Serves in the Austrian army in World War I. Taken prisoner and around this time begins work on his first book, *Tractatus Logico-Philosophicus*.

1921 *Tractatus Logico-Philosophicus* is published. Trains as a school teacher and starts teaching in Austria.

1926 Builds a house for his sister along with another architect, Paul Engelmann.

The Wittgenstein Haus, in Vienna

1929 Returns to Cambridge and resumes his work in philosophy.

1939 Becomes a professor at Cambridge University.

1951 Dies of cancer. His second book, *Philosophical Investigations*, is published two years after his death.

Ludwig Wittgenstein

"The limits of my language mean the limits of my world."

Ludwig Wittgenstein's books on logic, thought, and language are considered among the **most influential works of 20th-century philosophy**. However, Wittgenstein wasn't a philosopher for his whole career. After publishing his first book, he gave up philosophy and did various jobs as an architect, teacher, and gardener. He then took up philosophy again, writing a second book, *Philosophical Investigations*.

Early life

Born into a wealthy family, Wittgenstein was the youngest of eight children, and remained close to his siblings throughout his life. Their father was a rich industrialist, but was demanding and difficult. Wittgenstein moved to England to study engineering, and later went to Cambridge to study mathematics and logic under the British philosopher Bertrand Russell (1872–1970). It was during this period that Wittgenstein first developed an interest in philosophy.

The Wittgensteins were great patrons of Viennese art and culture.

Language and the world

The *Tractatus Logico-Philosophicus* was Wittgenstein's first major work. He wrote it while he was serving as a soldier in World War I. It deals with language, logic, and the connection between language and the world. Wittgenstein said that we can only talk or write about things that we can experience. He explained that statements have no real meaning if the words do not have a clear connection with things we experience in the world around us.

Later life

Wittgenstein believed that he had solved all the problems of philosophy in his first book, so he gave up philosophy for a time. But in 1929 he returned to Cambridge, where he began writing a book, *Philosophical Investigations*, that was published after his death. In this book he took a very different view of language—that we use language in many ways, not just logically or scientifically. He said that each different use of language has its own rules and procedures.

Wittgenstein was first a student and then a Professor of Philosophy at Trinity College, Cambridge.

The meaning of words

Wittgenstein devised the "beetle in a box" thought experiment to explore the relationship between words and objects, and between public and private language. Imagine that there are several people, and each one has a box with something (or maybe nothing) inside. Everyone refers to the contents of his or her box with the word "beetle." No one can look inside another person's box. Each person "knows" what a beetle is by looking inside his or her own box. "Beetle" cannot be the name of a thing, because each box contains something different. For each person the meaning of "beetle" is "the thing in my box." How is it we know what they call "beetle"?

Beetle

How do I know if I'm awake *or* dreaming?

People have always been fascinated by dreams. Just like thinking, dreaming occurs in our minds, but it only happens when we are asleep. **In our dreams, we see and hear things that are not actually happening**, but they seem real to us at the time. If dreams feel real, then how do we know when we are awake and when we are dreaming?

Imagination

We don't have to be asleep to experience things in our minds that are not real or happening to us in that moment. We have memories of things that have happened in the past, and can use our imagination to create new ideas. Unlike dreams, we have control over our imagination. But we can let our imagination wander, and sometimes this allows us to have new and inspiring ideas.

Mythical creatures, such as the phoenix, are created in our imaginations.

The way we experience feelings and emotions in our dreams can feel very real.

Dreams

In dreams we see, hear, and touch things, and even feel emotions in the same way as when we are awake. However, we can also experience some very strange things, since the rules of the real world do not apply— for example, we can fly, see monsters, and talk in many languages. Our brains don't think logically when we're asleep, and we cannot control our dreams.

Unconscious or asleep?

American philosopher Norman Malcolm (1911–90) pointed out a problem with the way we think about dreaming. He said we are aware of what we are dreaming, and we know we only dream when we are asleep. But if we are asleep, how can we be aware? And if we are conscious, we can't be asleep. Scientists have answered this question by explaining that in some stages of sleep we are not unconscious, but almost awake, and can be aware of our dreams.

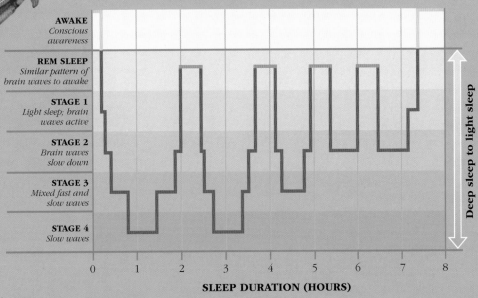

AWAKE
Conscious awareness

REM SLEEP
Similar pattern of brain waves to awake

STAGE 1
Light sleep; brain waves active

STAGE 2
Brain waves slow down

STAGE 3
Mixed fast and slow waves

STAGE 4
Slow waves

Deep sleep to light sleep

0 1 2 3 4 5 6 7 8
SLEEP DURATION (HOURS)

At night, we go through several stages of deep and light sleep. In deep sleep, our minds slow down, but they become active again in periods of light sleep (REM sleep), which is when we have dreams.

KEY
Awake
REM sleep
Non-REM sleep

Another reality?

It often seems like our dreams take us into another world. Scientists say that when we are dreaming we are not unconscious, but experiencing a different kind of consciousness. The things that happen in our dreams seem real, and we only recognize them as dreams when we wake up. But does this mean they are not real, or are they another kind of reality?

If you dream you are a superhero, could it in some way be real?

Dreaming differently

Zhuang Zhou's dream
The Chinese philosopher Zhuang Zhou (369–286 BCE) told a story of a dream he once had. He dreamed he was a butterfly. In the dream, the butterfly didn't know that it was really Zhuang Zhou. When he woke up, he was Zhuang Zhou again. But as he thought about it, he could not be sure if he was a man who had just dreamed he was a butterfly, or a butterfly that was now dreaming it was a man. He said that when we dream, we do not know we are dreaming. We only know that we were dreaming when we wake up.

Zhuang Zhou thought that perhaps life is a dream, and one day we will wake up and realize that it is not real.

How do blind people dream?
Most people only remember the things that they see in their dreams. But people who have been blind from birth have never experienced sight, so they dream about things they can hear, touch, and smell. Both blind and sighted people feel emotions in their dreams, such as fear or happiness, and sensations such as falling. This is because our dreams are based on the way we experience things when we are awake.

What is **happiness?**

All kinds of things can make us happy. We get pleasure from eating and drinking, or being warm and comfortable. We also get pleasure from doing our favorite things, for example, playing games or reading. **Sometimes it makes us happy to help others** and to know that we are doing good. Then there are the things that spoil happiness, such as pain, sadness, or fear—but we can be happy again if we overcome them.

Do good things

Many ancient Greek philosophers believed that we can only be truly happy if we lead a good life. They didn't think it was enough just to do the things we enjoy. We must also do things that are good and right. This gives us a different kind of pleasure. It makes us feel comfortable about how we live our lives and content with what we do.

Indian statesman Gandhi (1869–1948) devoted his life to doing good things.

Finding pleasure

Everyone wants to live a good life and be happy. The Greek philosopher Epicurus said that pleasure and pain are the way we can measure good and bad. Things that we like are good, and those that hurt us are bad. To lead a good life, we must look for what gives us pleasure and try to avoid anything that brings us pain and suffering.

Epicurus thought our goal in life should be to find the most enjoyment with the least pain.

Be satisfied

Some philosophers say that happiness comes from satisfying desires, such as eating something when we are hungry or meeting friends if we are feeling lonely. Others believe that real happiness comes not from these individual desires, but from being satisfied with life as a whole.

The simple life

A group of Greek philosophers called the Stoics thought that to find happiness we should lead a simple and natural life. They believed it is wrong to look for pleasure by becoming rich, famous, or powerful. We must also learn to accept that there are things that we can do nothing about. So we must look for the good things that happen, and not let the bad ones spoil our happiness.

Many people find happiness in family life, and in living and working with nature.

Dangerous sports like skydiving can be very exciting.

Thrill-seeking

The things that make us happy are not always what you might imagine. What some people find frightening, others enjoy as thrilling. Many of us like to feel frightened or excited sometimes, too. We may enjoy scary movies, or dangerous sports. Even if we have a tough experience we can enjoy the challenge and feel a sense of achievement at overcoming our fears or doing something difficult.

Experiencing unhappiness

We would all like to be happy all the time, but this isn't always possible. It is normal to feel pain when we are hurt, and to be sad when something bad happens. We may value happiness more if we know what it is like to be unhappy. Perhaps we need to experience every kind of feeling to live a full life.

The experience machine

Philosopher Robert Nozick (1938–2002) asked whether we really want to feel pleasure all the time. Suppose you could float in a tank, he said, that was warm and comfortable and protected you from everything unpleasant. Then you are connected to a machine that makes your brain think that you are experiencing nice things, such as eating chocolate or walking in a field of flowers. Would you choose the "experience machine" rather than real life, where things are not always so nice?

Why *do* people suffer?

No one likes to feel pain or unhappiness. But **we all suffer at some point in our lives**, and there are always people somewhere in the world who are suffering. Some suffering is caused by people, and some by nature. There are some kinds of suffering that we can do something to stop, but it seems the world can never be free of it. Perhaps suffering is as natural a part of our lives as happiness?

Good and evil

Our ideas of good and evil are connected with what gives us pleasure or pain. We think that something is good if it brings happiness, and evil if it causes unhappiness or suffering. When we say that someone is evil, it may be because he or she hurts other people or takes things from others that they need. But other things in the world cause suffering, too, such as floods and earthquakes. Is it right to call them "evil"?

When there is a natural disaster such as an earthquake, people with religious beliefs often ask why God has allowed it to happen.

The problem of evil

Many people believe in God. They think that God is good, loving, and has the power to do anything. But terrible things happen in the world, and there are bad people. Why would God let this happen? If God were good, he would want to prevent evil things. If he were all-powerful, he would be able to stop evil things from happening. So if God is good and all-powerful, why is there suffering in the world?

The best possible world

The German philosopher Gottfried Leibniz (1646–1716) tried to answer the problem of evil. He said that God chose to create this world. Since God is all-powerful, he could have chosen to make any world that he wanted. And because he is good, he chose the best world that it is possible to make. So, the world we live in must be the best possible world. If there is suffering in the best possible world, then it cannot be possible to have a world without suffering.

Even in the best possible world there will always be things that cause suffering, such as volcanic eruptions.

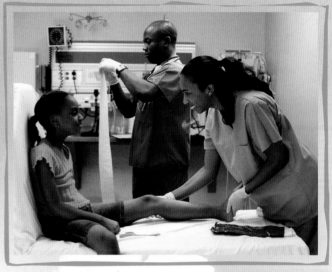

A nurse finds satisfaction in helping to ease suffering, and her patient is happy to find relief from her pain.

Is suffering necessary?

Many people believe that suffering cannot be avoided. But there are also some philosophers who think that it is necessary, that there is a reason for us to suffer. Helping others with their suffering, and learning to overcome our own suffering, can help us find meaning in our lives. Suffering can give us something to fight against, and it gives us something to contrast our happiness with. Without suffering, perhaps we wouldn't value our happiness.

Should punishment involve suffering?

When someone does something bad, it is often something that harms someone else and makes that person suffer in some way. Usually, we think they should be punished for what they have done wrong. But is it right for us to make someone suffer, even if they have caused suffering themselves? For example, many people think that it is wrong to smack a child if he is behaving badly, even if he has hurt someone else. But how should we punish criminals? Should they suffer, or is it enough to put them in prison?

What is infinity?

The earliest Greek philosophers looked at the stars in the sky and wondered about the shape of the universe. Does it have an edge? Did it have a beginning? Will it have an end? Or perhaps the universe has no edges, has always existed, and will never end. It is hard to imagine that **some things are endless or infinite**. Many philosophers have tried to understand the nature of infinity.

Counting forever

Plato and Aristotle noticed that there is more than one kind of infinity. We can go on adding to a series of numbers such as 1, 2, 3... and it will never be complete. This is a kind of infinity that has no end. But there is a different kind of infinity that can exist within boundaries. For example, there is an infinite number of divisions between 0 and 1. We can divide 1 by 2, and then again, and again, an endless number of times, but we will never reach an answer of 0.

A Möbius strip is a never-ending loop with only one edge and one surface. It helps us imagine one kind of infinity.

Could a monkey write like Shakespeare?

If you gave a monkey a keyboard, the chances of it writing something sensible are very small. Perhaps, by accident, it would type a word. But if it continued hitting the keys at random for long enough, other words would appear. Some philosophers argue that given an infinite amount of time, eventually the monkey would type Shakespeare's *Hamlet*.

The rope trick

Nothing can be longer than something infinitely long. Suppose you have the end of a rope in your hand, and it stretches out to infinity. It is infinitely long. But suppose you have the end of an identical rope in your other hand. That's infinitely long, too. Now, if you tie the ends together, how long is the knotted rope? Twice as long? Or infinitely long? Is there a difference between an infinite rope with a beginning, and an infinite rope that has no beginning and no end?

Endless arguments

When we use logical reasoning to show if something is true or false, we back up our argument with evidence. But sometimes we need to show that this evidence is true, too, with another argument and different evidence. Then we have to show this evidence is true, too, and so on. The process is never-ending, and is known as "infinite regress."

When two mirrors face each other, they reflect each other back and forth endlessly.

How do I decide what's right?

We make choices throughout our lives about what are **the right and wrong things** to do. We must decide what we think is good and bad. Sometimes, making a decision is harder than you might expect.

Who says what's right or wrong?

Most of the time, we know the difference between good and bad behavior without thinking about it. But philosophers are interested in how we know what is right and wrong. Teachers, the police, and the government use **rules and laws to tell us what to do and not to do**, but how do they know? Is there something about all the things that are right and good that makes them good?

Religious rules

Many people believe that God decides what is right and wrong. In most of the major religions, the holy books contain rules about what is virtuous and sinful, good and bad. For example, in the Christian Bible and Jewish Torah there are the Ten Commandments, and in the Quran there are the rules of sharia—code of the Islamic law. Many countries have social laws that originally come from religious laws. But are laws right because we believe God gave them to us? Or have these laws remained the same over the years because they are right?

According to the Bible, God wrote the Ten Commandments on stone tablets, which he gave to Moses.

The rule of law

In most countries today, laws are decided by governments. Most governments are elected by the people of the country to make laws for the society in which they live. So the laws are based on what most people think is right and wrong, such as laws against murder and theft. It is the job of the legal system to see that laws are applied fairly.

It's all relative

Different cultures have different ideas of what is right and wrong. For example, in some places it is usual for a man to have more than one wife, but this is against the law in most countries. What is right and wrong is not the same for everyone, and laws can change with time. Some philosophers say that what is good or bad is relative, depending on where and when you live.

In Myanmar's Kayan tribe, it is common for young girls to wear rings to stretch their necks. Many other societies think this is cruel.

Do we need rules?

We are taught rules and laws as we mature and learn what things are right and wrong. But we are also taught to think about why certain behavior is good or bad. Some philosophers say that we have a natural sense of what is good and bad and can decide this for ourselves. So do we really need rules?

Children are taught to reflect on why some behavior is bad.

Are some things always wrong?
Although different cultures have different customs and laws, most countries have similar laws against murder, stealing, and hurting other people. But while everyone agrees that fighting is wrong, most people agree it would be acceptable to fight to protect your family if it were in danger. If it's all right to fight in some situations, perhaps other things we think are bad can sometimes be right?

Right and wrong over time

Our ideas of right and wrong are not the same as they used to be. Some things that were once normal seem cruel or unfair to us now. Buying and selling people and forcing them to work seems completely wrong to us today. But it was accepted as normal for much of history, even in civilizations as far back as ancient Greece and Rome. There are now international laws against slavery.

Plantation owners in the United States bought African slaves to work in the fields in the 17th, 18th, and 19th centuries.

Second-class citizens
Throughout most of history, women have been treated unfairly. They did not have the same rights as men, such as being able to vote, own property, be educated, or pursue a profession. Campaigns by the suffragettes of the late 19th and early 20th centuries and the feminists of the 1960s and 70s helped to win equal rights for women in Europe and the United States. In some parts of the world, women are still do not have the right to vote.

Are some things wrong now?
Perhaps in the future, people will look back at things we do today and wonder how we could be so wrong. For example, many people eat meat, but others are becoming vegetarian—maybe a hundred years from now it will be thought wrong to breed animals for food. We are already beginning to see the dangers of some of our actions, such as dumping waste and cutting down rain forests.

Why *am* I here?

Many philosophers think about the purpose of life and what it means to be a living person. Some believe this matters more than trying to answer questions about the world around us. The philosophers called Existentialists say that **we should determine for ourselves what we want to be**. They suggest that each of us has a choice when it comes to deciding what is the right thing to do, and we must all take responsibility for our actions.

Not so ordinary

It can be hard to decide for ourselves what to do in life. Other people, such as governments, teachers, and parents may tell us what is right and wrong. German philosopher Friedrich Nietzsche (1844–1900) thought we should make our own choices, live life to the full, and be a "Superman" rather than an ordinary person. He said people who do this can become great artists, thinkers, or powerful leaders like Napoleon.

Napoleon Bonaparte

Scary possibilities

The Danish philosopher Søren Kierkegaard (1813–1855) believed that when we have to make up our minds about something, we are free to choose what we like. We must take responsibility for what we do. But knowing that anything is possible can be frightening. It is like the scary feeling you have when you stand on the edge of a cliff. You may feel a strange urge to jump off, but, of course, you don't have to. The choice is yours.

Edmund Husserl (1859–1938)

We can't know everything

A new kind of philosophy developed from the ideas of Edmund Husserl. This German thinker argued that there are some things we can never know. He thought philosophy ought to be about what we can know and see for ourselves. Husserl's philosophy made people pay more attention to what it is like to be alive, instead of worrying about mysterious, abstract things.

Being you

Think about what it is like to be you. It will soon become clear that you are different from anyone else. We each have our own special life, which has a beginning and an end. That thought might make us feel anxious and uncomfortable. However, it can also make us determined to live in the way we think best.

Life is time

It is how we experience being alive that interested German philosopher Martin Heidegger (1889–1976). He explained that between birth and death we see our lives as the passing of time. Life "flows" from the past to the present and into the future. Heidegger thought that "being" and "time" are the same thing.

Sisyphus had to roll a rock uphill for eternity.

Doing our own thing

It is up to us to choose between two different kinds of life. This is what French philosopher Jean-Paul Sartre (1905–1980) believed. He said that one choice is to live in the way that everyone in our society is expected to do. The other choice is to be the kind of person who feels right for us, and to live the life that suits us best.

We can choose to be different from everyone else.

What does it all mean?

For Sartre, knowing who we are gives us a chance to live how we want and find meaning in life. Another French philosopher, Albert Camus (1913–1960), had a gloomier view. He said life has no meaning, whatever we do. It seemed to him as pointless as the task given to Sisyphus, a king whose story is told in a Greek myth. In the Underworld, Sisyphus has to push a rock up a hill only to watch it roll back down, over and over again, forever.

Should we judge actions by their outcomes?

Many philosophers have tried to find ways of judging whether an action is right or wrong. Some suggest that we can make rules that tell us what is good and what is bad. But others say that it is not so simple. **To decide if something is morally right, we must look at what will happen if we do it**, and whether that outcome is good or bad.

English folklore character Robin Hood is considered a hero because he robbed the rich to give to the poor. But was he right to break the law?

Rules or outcomes?

There are certain rules about what is right and wrong, and usually we shouldn't break them. But perhaps what makes something good or bad is the effect it has, not the action itself. Is it what you do, or the result of what you do that really matters? Whenever we make a decision about what is the right thing to do, perhaps we should consider how the outcome will affect other people, instead of just following the rules without questioning them.

Do the ends justify the means?

Does it matter what we do or what means we use, as long as the outcome is good in the end? We have to look at all the consequences. For example, it might be right to let one person die to save 100 lives, but wrong to kill 100 to save just one. Perhaps we need to look at people's intentions, too. Did they do something bad because they knew it would have good consequences, or was it just a bad thing that turned out fine in the end?

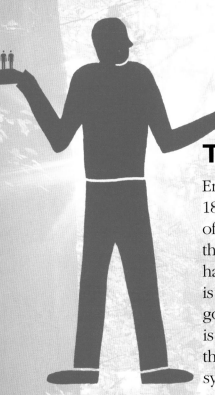

The greatest happiness

English philosopher Jeremy Bentham (1748–1832) believed that we can decide the morality of an action by looking at its outcome. He said that what matters is how much happiness or harm the action causes. To judge whether it is right or wrong, we have to weigh all the good and bad consequences. He argued that "it is the greatest happiness of the greatest number that is the measure of right and wrong"—a system that became known as utilitarianism.

Pursuing happiness

Bentham based his system on "happiness," meaning all the things that give us pleasure, such as food, shelter, and doing the things we enjoy. Other philosophers said we should be free to live our lives in the pursuit of happiness, but remember that we all have different ideas of what gives us pleasure.

Playing computer games is pleasurable for some people, but it is not everyone's idea of happiness.

The harm principle

We must think about the impact of our actions on other people. English philosopher John Stuart Mill (1806–73) said that something is good if it gives pleasure to other people, but that it is not wrong to do things that make us happy, too. He argued that something is only wrong if it harms someone else, or stops them from doing what brings them happiness. In addition to the happiness caused by our actions, we must consider the "harm principle"— how much our actions hurt other people or interfere with their happiness.

You may enjoy listening to loud music in public, but other people might find it annoying.

Outcomes through the ages

Epicurus

Ancient Greek philosophers tried to discover what we mean by good or bad. Epicurus suggested that things that cause pain are bad, and things that cause pleasure are good. He said an action is morally right if it causes the least possible pain and the most possible pleasure.

In ancient Greece, the god Dionysus was associated with things that give pleasure, such as food and parties.

Niccolò Machiavelli

Machiavelli was an adviser to rulers in Renaissance Italy. He argued that sometimes it is right for a leader to do terrible things, such as lying and killing, for the good of his people, even if he knows he is doing wrong.

Cesare Borgia was the kind of ruler that Machiavelli described—Borgia was cunning and ruthless in pursuit of what he thought was the greater good.

Utilitarianism

Bentham's utilitarianism, the idea that a good action is one that brings the most happiness, inspired many others. Austrian-British philosopher Karl Popper (1902–94) changed the original idea to say that the measure of right or wrong is not the greatest happiness, but the least pain.

93

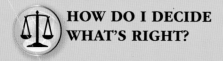
How should I act?

Consequences

One way to judge whether what we do is right or wrong is by weighing up the amount of pleasure or pain our behavior produces. This outcome is known as the "consequence" of the action. We can decide how to behave by choosing actions that have the best outcomes for the most people. This system is not based on hard and fast rules, such as "killing is wrong." Instead, we must consider the consequences of everything we do.

Sometimes making a decision is a question of balancing the consequence of either choice.

Not black and white

However, it is not always easy to decide what is the best outcome of our actions. Often we don't have time to weigh up all the possible outcomes of what we might do. Sometimes, our personal feelings affect our decisions, and other people may see things differently.

The **streetcar problem**

Choosing the right thing to do can often be difficult. Some philosophers believe you should choose to do whatever gives the most happiness to the most people. But even this is not simple. In this problem, British philosopher Philippa Foot shows that decisions are more than just a matter of numbers.

An empty streetcar has broken loose and is speeding out of control down a railroad track. Farther down the line, five people are tied to the tracks. The streetcar will run them over. There is no way of stopping it, but there is a lever nearby. By pulling the lever you can send the streetcar down a different track. However, there is one other person tied to the tracks on the other line. What do you do?

If you pull the lever, you save five lives, but the other person gets run over. If you do nothing, you will let five people die. But they would be run over anyway if you hadn't been there. On the other hand, if you pull the lever, you have deliberately made the decision to kill one person. Is killing someone any different from allowing someone to die?

The hands-on approach

In another version of the streetcar problem, there is only one railroad line. There is a man standing on a bridge over the track. If you push him off the bridge, he will land in front of the streetcar, stopping it. You can save the five people tied to the track, but the man you push will die. Should you push him? Would pushing him off the bridge be different from pulling the lever? What if he were the person who tied the five people to the tracks in the first place— would that affect your decision?

A friend in danger

Just as in the original streetcar problem, you can save five people by pulling a lever. This time, however, you recognize the single person tied to the second railroad track. Would your decision change if this person were your friend or a member of your family? You might think letting five strangers die is worth it to save someone important to you. Would you feel differently if the person were someone you think is bad, such as a thief or murderer?

Think about it!

The balloon

Suppose you are in a group of people riding in a hot-air balloon. It beomes clear that the balloon's load is too heavy, and you begin slowly falling toward the sea. The sea is full of hungry sharks. To make the balloon lighter, you need to get rid of one of the passengers. One person must be thrown to the sharks to save everyone else. But how do you choose who to throw out? It might be a good idea to choose the heaviest. Or do you choose the oldest? Perhaps one of the passengers is a doctor, and another a criminal. Would that affect your decision? Is one person more valuable than another? Would you jump yourself to let the other passengers live?

Telling tales

Three of your friends are in trouble at school. The teacher believes they wrote a dirty poem on the restroom wall. You know they didn't do it, but you don't know who did. To get them out of trouble, you could tell the teacher that Ann, the meanest girl in the class, did it—and you're sure the teacher would believe you. Your three innocent friends wouldn't be punished for something they didn't do, but Ann would be. What's the right thing to do?

The runaway streetcar will run over five people unless someone pulls the lever. Should you kill one person to save the others?

Biography

1724 Born in Königsberg, Prussia (now Kaliningrad, Russia).

1734 Goes to school at the Collegium Fredericianum, one of the best schools in Königsberg.

1740 Enrolls at the University of Königsberg to study mathematics and philosophy.

1746 When his father dies, he finishes his studies to earn a living as a private tutor, but also writes about philosophy and astronomy.

1755 Returns to the University of Königsberg, where he receives a Master's degree and becomes a lecturer.

1770 Is appointed Professor at the University of Königsberg.

1781 Publishes his most famous work, *Critique of Pure Reason*.

1792 King Frederick William II bans him from lecturing about religious subjects.

1797 Retires from his job at the University, but continues writing.

1804 Dies in Königsberg, at the age of 79. His last words are "It is good."

Inspired many

Kant wrote books on all aspects of philosophy, and he developed a system of philosophy that was revolutionary. Although his work is very difficult to read and understand, his ideas inspired many other philosophers in his lifetime, and they formed the basis for German philosophy in particular for more than 100 years.

Immanuel Kant

"Human reason is troubled by questions that it cannot dismiss, but also cannot answer."

Born in Prussia, Kant was raised in a strict, religious family. He did well in school, and, at just 16, he went to the University of Königsberg, where he later became a Professor of Logic and Metaphysics. He devoted his life to teaching and writing about philosophy, becoming **one of the most influential philosophers of the 18th century**.

Using reason

Unlike many philosophers of his time, Kant believed that knowledge of what is right and wrong is not something that exists in nature, or is given to us by God. He argued that we decide what is morally right for ourselves by using reason. Instead of judging the morality of an action by its outcome, Kant thought we should have unbreakable rules of morality. If we think something is wrong, then it must be wrong for everyone, at all times.

Kant developed his influential ideas in discussions with a circle of friends and followers.

This woodcut shows a man looking outside the world he experiences with his senses.

Two worlds

Kant said that we know about things through our senses. But we cannot experience things as they actually are—we only know what we can see, touch, hear, and so on. He said there are two different worlds—the world of things as we experience them, and another world that we do not have any way of experiencing, and therefore that we cannot know.

How do we know the world?

In his most important book, *Critique of Pure Reason*, Kant draws connections between reason, rational thinking, and experience, to show how we learn about the world. He introduced ideas that changed the way people thought about philosophy, and it immediately made him famous.

Kant's *Critique of Pure Reason*, published in 1781.

Should you *ever* tell a lie?

Most people agree that it is important to tell the truth and that it is wrong to lie. Some people never tell lies because they feel it is always wrong, whatever the circumstance. There are, however, times when many people think that it is acceptable to lie, for example, if it stops someone from feeling hurt. But **are there times when it is acceptable to break a moral rule?**

White lies

Not all lies are the same—some lies are serious and obviously wrong, and other lies do very little harm. There are even "white lies"—lies that we tell to protect people, or to avoid hurting their feelings. For example, you might say that the ugly sweater your aunt gave you for your birthday is just what you wanted. Is it really wrong to tell a lie like that?

If you visit a friend's house and are served a meal you don't like, should you say you don't like it, or lie and say how delicious it is?

Always bad

Some philosophers argue that if something is bad, it will always be bad. They say we must make rules about what is good and bad and stick to them. German philosopher Immanuel Kant said that we should only make rules that we think should become unbreakable rules. If we decide that lying is wrong in one case, it must always be wrong, for everyone. Even white lies are not acceptable.

As a boy, US president George Washington chopped down a cherry tree. When his father asked who had chopped down the tree, George admitted it. He was forgiven by his father because he had not lied.

One rule for me

If moral rules should never be broken, when something is good in one case, it must be good in all cases. You cannot have one rule for yourself and a different one for everyone else. Some philosophers say that you should not tell a lie unless you agree that it's all right for everyone to tell lies all the time. But then no one would ever know who was telling the truth! Perhaps it is better to say that it is always wrong to tell lies.

This girl thinks it's acceptable to lie if she keeps her fingers crossed, but how does she know that others aren't doing the same thing?

The golden rule
We often judge whether an action is good or bad by the effect it has on other people. One way of looking at this is to put yourself in someone else's place. A number of philosophers, and many religions, say that there is a golden rule, "do as you would be done by." When we do something that affects other people, we should do what we would like them to do if it affected us. If you wouldn't want someone to lie to you, then you shouldn't lie to anyone yourself.

The snowball effect

One argument against allowing exceptions to a rule is that it can lead to a "snowball effect," where things go from bad to worse. For example, a small lie that seems harmless at first can lead to more lies, and gradually the lies might become bigger and more serious. Where do we draw the line between an acceptable lie and one that is not acceptable? Perhaps it is better never to lie at all, even if this means that sometimes people's feelings get hurt.

Could I have chosen something different?

We spend a lot of time and effort making decisions and trying to make the best choices we can. But **how much freedom of choice do we really have**? Some philosophers say that we have free will to make whatever choices we want, but that we must take responsibility for our actions. Others believe that our choices and actions are dictated for us by circumstances or by a higher being.

Free will

Choosing what is the right thing to do and taking responsibility for what we choose seems to be an essential part of leading a good life. But if a good and all-powerful god exists, would he let us make bad choices or do evil things? Some Christian philosophers say that free will is a gift from God. He allows us to have the power to choose for ourselves, even though he knows that we will not always choose what is good.

Are we free to make our own choices?

An illusion

Other people think that free will is an illusion. They say that circumstances such as our upbringing, culture, and the opinions of others shape our character, and our character determines what we do. Some take this idea even further and believe that everything we do is determined for us. They say that even when we think we are making a choice, our decision is unavoidable— we could never have decided anything different.

Some people say that our actions inevitably follow each other, like one domino making the next one fall, and so on.

No power to choose

People who believe that our actions are caused, or determined, by other things are known as determinists. Some, the hard determinists, say that we have no free will at all. They say that because we have no power over what we decide to do, we are not responsible for our actions. Others, the soft determinists, believe that it is only the choices that are mapped out for us, not the outcomes. We still have the freedom to act differently, so can be held responsible.

The riders on a ski lift are like people without free will, they can travel in one direction only. But people skiing down the mountain can choose their own direction.

Nature versus nurture

Some people believe that the most important influence on our moral choices is our character, or "nature." They say that we inherit our way of behaving—it is something we are born with. Others believe that the way we behave is something we learn. Outside influences, such as what we are taught and our upbringing, or "nurture," are most important in determining how we act.

Are our actions programmed in our DNA, or is our behavior also shaped by our environment?

Making choices

The locked room
The 17th-century English philosopher John Locke believed that free will is just an illusion. To illustrate this, he used the idea of a man locked alone in a room. The man is asleep and someone locks the room from the outside. The man does not know that he has been locked in. When he wakes up, he decides to stay in the room. The man thinks he has the freedom to choose to remain in the room or go out as he pleases. But really he has no freedom to choose because the door to the room is locked.

Are we all like the man in John Locke's room who does not realize that he has no freedom to make a choice?

Does God know what we are going to do?
In most religions God is described as "omniscient," meaning all-knowing. Those who believe in God believe that he knows everything that has happened and everything that will happen. But if God knows what we will do next, do we really have a choice or free will? One answer to this question is that even though he knows what will happen, God still gives us the freedom to choose. Danish philosopher Søren Kierkegaard (1813–55) said that God would create us as free beings, because the greatest good he could do for us would be to make us free.

Difficult choices

Problems of what is right and wrong don't just concern philosophers. We all face ethical dilemmas—difficult choices about what is the correct thing to do. **Making the right decision is important to the way we feel**, even in small, day-to-day situations. Philosophy can help us make decisions about what we should and shouldn't do. How would you react to the situations described here?

Should I tell the teacher?

You have just moved into a new class at school and find that everyone is getting better grades than you in the weekly tests. You find out that all the students have been cheating. You don't want to cheat like them, but if you don't, you will be at the bottom of the class. If you tell the teacher that the others are cheating, then everyone in the class will dislike you. Should you keep quiet and do your best? Should you cheat? Or should you tell the teacher?

Should I take the money?

You are walking down the street and notice there is some money sticking out of a cash machine. Someone has obviously forgotten to take it. But there is no one in sight, so you do not know who it belongs to. You could hand it in at the bank, but it is not the bank's money—it belongs to the person who forgot to take it. If you take the money, no one will ever know. Besides, if you don't, someone else is bound to. You know it is wrong to steal, but would this really be stealing?

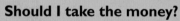

Should I lie?

A bully at school is angry. Someone has damaged his bike. He and his friends think you know who did it. They come over and start to push you around. You tell them the truth—you don't know who it was. Unfortunately, the bully doesn't believe you. He says that if you don't tell him who did it, they will beat up your younger brother. Should you give the bully a name to stop your brother from being hurt? Whose name? Perhaps you should say that you did it?

Should I call the police?

You have just seen a man robbing a bank. You follow him and see him give the stolen money to the manager of an orphanage. The manager doesn't know the money is stolen. He thanks the robber and tells him that without the money the orphanage would have to close. You recognize the robber. You could tell the police but if they arrest him they will give the money back to the bank. Is it all right to say nothing so the orphanage can use the money?

Should I admit it?

One day, a friend of yours leaves her phone at your house. You notice it is switched on and not locked. You look through her messages, even though you know they are private, and discover that she has been saying awful things about you to her other friends. You are very hurt and upset and want to tell her that you think she has behaved badly. But if you do, you will have to own up to looking at her private messages. What should you do?

Should I cut the rope?

You are climbing a mountain with friends when there is a rock fall. The person below you has been knocked off the cliff face and is hanging on a rope. Her weight stops you and the person above you from climbing to safety. You are all in danger from another rock fall. If you cut the rope, the fall will kill your friend, but you and your other friend will be able to escape. If you don't cut the rope, you may all be killed by falling rocks before someone can come to rescue you. How do you choose which lives to save?

Shouldn't men and women *be* equal?

In almost every culture throughout history, women have been treated differently from men. Traditionally, it was thought that "a woman's place is in the home." Certain types of career and job were not open to women at all. It is only in the last 100 years that this has changed in some countries and women have started to enjoy equal rights, including the right to vote in elections. Will women ever be treated the same way as men?

No freedom for women

In the ancient world, it was taken for granted in most cultures that a man was the head of the household, while the women in his family had to do as he said. Times moved on and societies changed, but women gained little or no freedom. Today, this unfair situation has improved in many parts of the world. Even so, in some countries women are still not treated equally.

Women such as politician Aung San Suu Kyi (1945–) of Myanmar are inspirational leaders in a world largely run by men.

The fight for equal rights

At the end of the 18th century, people in the US and France overthrew their royal rulers and set up fairer societies. Citizens were given certain rights, such as the right to vote, which were written down in documents such as the French *Declaration of the Rights of Man and the Citizen*. But only men had all these rights, not women. The French writer Olympe de Gouges (1748–93) responded with her own *Declaration of the Rights of Women,* which demanded equal rights for women. In England, writer Mary Wollstonecraft (1759–97) campaigned for equal rights for women, especially the right to education.

The Statue of Liberty in New York represents Libertas, the female goddess of freedom.

WOMEN'S SOCIAL AND POLITICAL UNION.

VOTES FOR WOMEN

W.S.P.U.

MARCH OF THE WOMEN
(Popular Edition in F...To be sung in Unison)
By ETHEL SMYTH, Mus.Doc.
Price: One Shilling & Sixpence net.
WOMAN'S PRESS, 156, Charing Cross Rd., London W.C. and BREITKOPF & HÄRTEL, 54, Gt. Marlborough St., London, W.

Margaret Morris 1911

Who can vote?

One of the most important human rights is to be able to vote—to have a say in the way society is governed. For most of history, only men could vote. In the 19th century, women began to demand this right for themselves. British philosopher Harriet Taylor (1807–58) and her husband, John Stuart Mill (1806–73), also a philosopher, headed a campaign to bring about a change in the law. This inspired a Women's Suffrage movement ("suffrage" means the right to vote) in Britain and elsewhere. Campaigners eventually won voting rights for women in many countries.

This 1911 songsheet shows the suffragettes marching for voting rights for women.

Why are most philosophers men?

Without education, it is difficult to learn about philosophy. It's even harder if you have little chance to get out and talk to people. For many centuries, most women didn't have a good education. They were also expected to stay at home most of the time. Of course, many women wondered about things in the same way as men, but often their ideas were not written down or passed on. However, since the 20th century, there has been an increasing number of women philosophers, such as French feminists Simone de Beauvoir (1908–86) and Luce Irigaray (1930–).

Different minds?

Men and women may have different bodies, but do they have different minds as well? Traditionally, careers were divided by gender. Jobs such as the armed forces and engineering were considered "male" jobs, and nursing and teaching were "female" jobs. Now such ideas seem very out of date. Is this because we no longer believe there is such a big difference between men and women? Perhaps people behave and think in a "male" or "female" way only because society expects them to.

Today, most people believe that men and women can do the same jobs equally well.

105

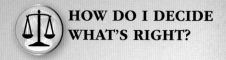
Biography

1908 Born in Paris, France.

1929 Graduates from the Sorbonne (the University of Paris) with a degree in philosophy.

De Beauvoir met the philosopher Jean-Paul Sartre in 1929. Their friendship lasted until he died in 1980.

1931 Begins teaching literature and philosophy, first in Marseille and later in Rouen.

1941-43 Professor at the Sorbonne, during the German occupation of Paris in World War II.

1943 Publishes her first novel, *She Came to Stay*.

1945 Joins the editorial staff of *Les Temps Modernes*, a journal of politics, philosophy, and literature.

1949 Publishes her best-known book, *The Second Sex*.

1986 Dies in Paris at the age of 78 and is buried in the cemetery in Montparnasse.

Simone de Beauvoir

"Be loved, be admired, be necessary; be somebody."

Philosopher, pioneer of feminism, teacher, and successful author: Simone de Beauvoir was all of these. She was born in Paris, where she lived and worked for most of her life. Whether sitting with friends in cafés or teaching students in college, de Beauvoir inspired people with her ideas about personal freedom.

Ahead of her time

When de Beauvoir was young, it was unusual for women to go to college and have a career. She was one of the first women to graduate from the Sorbonne, the best university in France. She was also the youngest person, at 21, to take the exclusive French civil service exam in philosophy. Later, she taught at the Sorbonne and was one of the first important female philosophers.

The Sorbonne—de Beauvoir was a student and later a Professor of Philosophy here.

Being female, being feminine

Simone de Beauvoir was an important influence on the modern feminist movement, which began in the last half of the 20th century. She argued that society expects women to behave in a particular way—to be feminine, and to be submissive and obedient. De Beauvoir said that there is a difference between being born female and becoming feminine by conforming to society's ideas of what a woman should be.

Moroccan women protest about violence against women in a demonstration outside the parliament in Morocco in 2013.

Not just a philosopher

Politics

Simone de Beauvoir was interested in politics and wrote a great deal about society and women's issues. With Jean-Paul Sartre (1905–1980) and other writers and thinkers, she helped set up a magazine, *Les Temps Modernes* (*Modern Times*), which she wrote articles for and edited.

Simone de Beauvoir at her writing desk.

Setting women free

De Beauvoir was an "existentialist" philosopher. This means that she believed people must find their own meaning in life. In her book *The Second Sex*, she said that society tells women how to behave, and has made them lower in rank than men. She thought women could choose to act differently and be what they want to be. At the time, this was an exciting new way of thinking.

In the 1960s and 1970s thousands of women demanded equality with men, encouraged by de Beauvoir's book *The Second Sex*.

Well-known writer

Like other French philosophers of the time, de Beauvoir was a respected author. In addition to books on philosophy, she wrote novels, including *The Mandarins*, which won an important literary prize, and short stories. She also published her travel diaries and an autobiography.

L'Invitée (*She Came to Stay*) was Simone de Beauvoir's first novel.

Why should we **care** about the **environment?**

The planet we live on provides us with all the resources we need, including food, water, and fuel. It is also home to many other living things. There is enough for us all to live on, but we need to manage our resources carefully. Scientists warn that **people are not taking good care of our environment**, and important parts of the world around us have been destroyed. But caring for the environment is not just a matter of science and technology—it also raises important philosophical questions.

In some cities there are so many cars that the air is not fit to breathe.

Doing damage

Humans are very inventive. We have developed all kinds of technology to make life easier and more comfortable for ourselves. But we are now finding that there is a downside to this. To provide energy for our transportation and to power our homes and factories, we burn fossil fuels such as coal, oil, and gas. This causes pollution and damages our environment. But is it right to ask people to give up the things that make their lives comfortable?

A fair share of resources

The Earth has all the resources we need, but they are not shared evenly. In some places people do not have enough food or water. In other places there is so much food that some of it is thrown away. Is it right to let some people starve while others live in comfort? Is there a way to share the world's resources fairly? As the population of the world grows, this problem will become more and more important.

Developed countries use most of the world's resources, leaving everyone else to share the rest. Is this fair?

A delicate balance

As our population grows, we need more and more food. Farmers have developed new ways to increase production of animals and crops. But sometimes modern methods of farming harm the environment. For example, forests are cut down to make way for fields of grain, and man-made fertilizers pollute rivers. Farms produce more, but other plants and animals can no longer live there. This may make things worse rather than better in the long run. Do we have a responsibility to protect the natural environment?

The insecticides that farmers use to prevent pests from eating their crops can also harm the bees that pollinate the fruit and vegetable plants.

Cleaner sources of energy such as wind or solar power are good for the environment in the long term.

Think like a mountain

Some philosophers believe we have a responsibility to all living things, and to the environment. Norwegian Arne Naess (1912–2009), one of the first environmental philosophers, said we should "think like a mountain." This means that we should behave as if we will always be here and think of the long-term consequences. We must remember that we are a part of nature, and stop trying to control it for our own advantage.

Impact on the future

Modern technology has made life better for most people, and even saved lives. But many agree that our technology is causing climate change and other negative consequences, which may be harmful in the future. The way we treat our environment has long-lasting effects. When making decisions, we have to think about not just the people alive today, but also about whether we are harming future people.

The way we treat our environment today may cause problems in the future, such as rising sea levels and extreme weather conditions.

Are humans *worth* more than animals?

Humans are just one of many species of animal on Earth. When we decide what is right and wrong, we try not to hurt other humans, but **sometimes we don't apply the same rules to other animals**. Some people think we are different from other animals, or even better than them. But does that mean we can use them to work for us and provide us with food? Do we have a responsibility to make sure we protect animals?

Battery chickens are squeezed into cages in conditions humans couldn't bear. Do they suffer in the same way we would?

The human animal

When Charles Darwin (1809–1882) explained his theory of evolution, saying that all humans come from apelike ancestors, people realized for the first time that humans are a species of animal. If we are just a kind of animal, then perhaps other animals are more like us than we thought. Later philosophers began to think about whether the way we treat animals is right. How would we feel if we were treated in the same way?

This killer whale is kept in captivity for our entertainment. Should it have a right to freedom?

Animal rights

Australian philosopher Peter Singer (1946–) said that to behave ethically, we must think about the effects of our actions on animals as well as people. Like humans, many animals have feelings and can suffer. We should consider whether what we do might hurt an animal, or cause it distress. Humans have laws to protect their right to live peacefully without being harmed by other people. Perhaps all animals should have rights, too.

We could feed more people by growing crops in this field than by using it to graze cattle for food.

Going vegetarian

Most people around the world eat meat. We are just one of the many animals that eat other animals. But we can live healthily without meat, and it is cheaper to grow crops than to raise farm animals. So, is it right to kill an animal just for food? If we believe that it is wrong to make animals suffer, perhaps we should all become vegetarians. Or is eating meat a natural part of the food chain?

Do animals know what's right?

Some people think we don't need to behave ethically toward animals, because animals don't behave ethically themselves. But do they have a sense of right and wrong, or what is fair and unfair? Some animals kill other animals without thinking about whether they suffer or not. Some animals fight and steal from one another. However, they do these things to protect their families and provide them with food. Animals do things that we think of as wrong, but maybe they are simply acting on instinct with no ability to reason about right or wrong.

Are all animals equal?

We do not think of all living things in the same way. For example, a vegetarian who thinks it is wrong to kill animals for food might think it is fine to swat a mosquito. Perhaps it is because some animals are more like us. But is it right to think that some animals deserve better treatment than others? For example, we wouldn't hurt a chimpanzee, but might squash an ant. Where do we draw the line?

When pests threaten our homes, most of us do not feel it is wrong to have the pests exterminated.

Animals in danger

Protected species

There are many kinds of animal and plant in the world that are becoming very rare. Some species, such as tigers, polar bears, and white rhinos, may soon disappear completely. To protect them from extinction, we have laws banning people from hunting them. But we still kill other animals for sport and for food. Is the life of a rare panda worth more than the life of a pig farmed for its meat?

Life is increasingly difficult for polar bears because the ice where they live is melting.

Extinction

It is sad when a species becomes extinct. Do we have a responsibility to save animal species? Sometimes it is the fault of humans that they are dying out. We have destroyed their natural homes or hunted them to extinction. But it is also natural for some species to survive and others to become extinct. By saving a species, are we interfering with nature?

The Thylacine, or Tasmanian wolf, lived in Australia and Tasmania. It became extinct in the early 1930s because farmers killed it to stop it from eating their livestock.

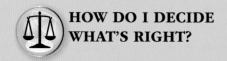

HOW DO I DECIDE WHAT'S RIGHT?

Giving more

Emergency aid

After a natural disaster, such as an earthquake or flood, people are often happy to give money to help those in need. But there are people in need all the time, not just after natural disasters.

People made homeless by wars or natural disasters often rely on donations from rich countries.

Foreign aid

The governments of rich countries try to help those in poor countries by sending money. Most give a small part of the country's wealth in foreign aid. However, people often do not donate themselves because their governments are providing aid. Don't we have individual responsibility for those in need?

Foreign aid from rich countries can help to provide food and clean water to people in poor countries.

Should we **save** the **drowning child?**

In general, we all feel that **it is right to help other people when they are in danger.** We have a responsibility to do what we can. It would be wrong not to do anything. We don't, however, always do as much as we could. To highlight this, Australian philosopher Peter Singer came up with the following thought experiment.

Imagine that you are walking to school, wearing a new pair of shoes that you have bought with your allowance. You walk past a pond and notice that a small girl has fallen in. She cannot swim. You know the pond is shallow and you could wade in and pull her to safety. But you must hurry and won't have time to take off your shoes. They will be ruined. Should you rescue the girl? Almost everyone will answer "Of course I should" if you were to ask this question. A child's life is obviously more important than a pair of shoes. But suppose there are other people by the pond. They could rescue the girl, but they are doing nothing. Do you still feel it is your responsibility to wade in and save her?

Now imagine that the child is in danger in a faraway country. You can't be there to rescue the child yourself. But giving some money can save the child's life. Should you give money to rescue the child?

You were happy to ruin your new shoes to save the drowning child, so perhaps you could give the price of a pair of shoes.

Now think about the real world. There are millions of children who do not have enough to eat, or who need medical treatment, but their families are too poor to pay for it. Millions of people live in rich countries and are able to afford luxuries, such as new shoes. If we are in the lucky position of being able to afford luxuries, should we feel obligated to give money to organizations that help save children's lives? Just as in the case of the child in the shallow pond, wealthy people can save lives without danger to themselves, and without spending much money. They would only have to give up a few luxuries. Don't we have the same obligation to give money as we had to save the drowning child?

Children all over the world are living in poverty and have to do dangerous work, such as sorting through garbage, to stay alive. Is it our duty to do more to help them?

Think about it!

What are your priorities?

In the drowning child story, nearly everyone would be happy to give up a pair of new shoes to save the child right in front of them. But what would you be prepared to go without to give something to an aid organization that helps children in another place? Could you go without buying yourself some candy, or skip a trip to the movies from time to time? It would not be a great hardship for you, but the cost of those treats could make a great difference to someone in a poor country. It is a question of priorities—what do you think is more important?

Why is it my responsibility?

Singer asks whether it makes a difference if there are other people by the pond who could help the drowning child but aren't doing anything. Would you also choose not to help because the people who are already there are doing nothing? In a similar way, we sometimes try to shift individual responsibility for helping to our governments. We think they should help people in poor countries, but they don't always do enough. Isn't it up to each of us to do what we can, rather than hope that someone else will?

Will there ever be world peace?

A hydrogen bomb, also known as an atom bomb, is a lethal nuclear weapon that can destroy entire cities in minutes.

History is filled with stories of wars. There has never been a time when there wasn't a conflict somewhere in the world. Battles are fought over land, for resources such as water or oil, or for political or religious beliefs. Yet most people don't want to be at war, and a growing number believe **it is possible to settle differences without fighting**. But is it sometimes necessary to defend your land and protect people by fighting? Perhaps there can never be an end to war.

Is war ever right?

Almost all religions say that killing and violence are wrong. But both Christian and Islamic philosophers have said that sometimes it is right to fight a war—what they call a "just war." They believe leaders should only take their countries to war for the good of their people once they have tried every other way of settling a conflict.

In the 12th and 13th centuries, Christian and Islamic armies fought for control of the Holy Land in Jerusalem.

Have nuclear weapons prevented war?

Nuclear bombs are the most destructive weapons ever invented. Several of the most powerful countries have nuclear weapons, but they know that if they use them, they will be attacked with nuclear weapons in return. Some people say that this knowledge has prevented wars. The only time a nuclear weapon has been used in conflict was against Japan at the end of World War II. Is the threat of the devastation that nuclear weapons would cause preventing another World War?

Is it in our nature?

Some people argue that there can never be peace in the world because fighting is part of our basic human nature. We fight to defend ourselves and our families, and attack others to take things when we need them. Others, pacifists, believe that fighting is always wrong and that war is not necessary. Humans have created societies with laws to prevent us from behaving like wild animals, and to help us resolve our differences without war. But there will always be some people who behave aggressively. Pacifists say that it is wrong to go to war with them and we should find a peaceful way of dealing with them. But is it possible not to fight back if someone attacks you?

International cooperation

One way to prevent wars is to make sure that countries can meet together and discuss their differences. Many countries agree to work together as a group, or in an alliance, to defend their people. Nearly every country in the world belongs to the United Nations (UN)—an international organization that works to prevent war and promote peace. There are also international laws to help decide right and wrong when there is a conflict. The UN has international armies to help keep the peace.

Soldiers from many countries work together in the United Nations peace-keeping force.

Peaceful protests

Antiwar demonstrations

In the last 100 years, there have been two World Wars, and many other wars on a smaller scale. Millions of people have experienced the horrors of war. Many people believe that there is no good reason to fight most wars and that the suffering they cause is not justified.

In the 21st century, hundreds of thousands of people all over the world have taken part in protests against war.

Nonviolence

When the leaders of a country make laws that treat people unfairly, it can lead to fighting and even war. Many people believe that there are ways of stopping unfairness without using violence. One way is to hold a demonstration—a meeting or a march—to protest peacefully against injustice. Another is to disobey the laws that you disagree with, or refuse to pay taxes to the government that is acting unfairly.

Martin Luther King led the movement for equal rights in the US using nonviolent protest.

Why do we need rules?

Rules help us to lead good lives and get along with other people. The problem is **how to decide what the rules should be**, and who should make them.

Are people naturally good *or* bad?

People usually live in groups, or societies. When we come together to form a society, we make rules about what the members of the group are allowed to do or not do. For example, laws against stealing or hurting other people help us live together safely and happily. But **would people steal and hurt one another if we didn't have laws**? Are people naturally bad? Or are we naturally good and helpful? If we are naturally good, why do we need laws?

In a lawless society, would people fight over food like wild animals?

The state of nature

The English philosopher Thomas Hobbes (1588–1679) had a low opinion of human nature. He believed that people are basically selfish and that their natural state is to fight for what they want without caring about others. Hobbes said that to make a civilized society people need laws that force them to behave well, and a strong leader to make sure they obey those laws.

The law of nature

Not all philosophers believe people are naturally selfish. John Locke thought that people are naturally good and like to cooperate. According to Locke, people instinctively follow the "law of nature" and treat each other well. He said we make laws in society based on this law of nature. Laws are made to protect our rights and help us to decide what is right when there is a dispute.

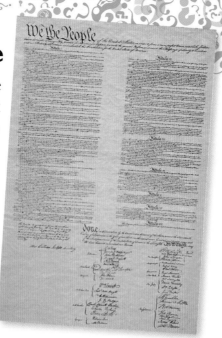

Locke would say that the Constitution of the United States of America echoes the law of nature.

In the French Revolution, the people took power from the ruling royalty because they wanted to decide how to live for themselves.

The will of the people

French philosopher Jean-Jacques Rousseau (1712–78) also believed that people are naturally good. But he believed that the laws of society stop us from behaving naturally. According to Rousseau, the laws are made by rulers to protect their property and do not allow most people to live freely. He said that the laws should be made by the people, according to the "general will," to give people the freedom to live as they want.

Living by the rules

Making the law

It is the job of the government to make laws. Usually governments are formed of politicians, who represent the people and are chosen in elections. In addition to national governments making laws for the whole country, there can be regional and local governments for smaller communities. Nearly every country in the world is a member of the United Nations, which makes international laws.

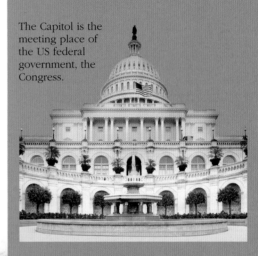

The Capitol is the meeting place of the US federal government, the Congress.

Breaking the law

Each country has slightly different laws, but some, such as laws against robbery and murder, are similar everywhere. Laws are made by governments, but it is the courts that decide if someone has broken a law. People who break the law can be punished by being sent to prison or made to pay fines.

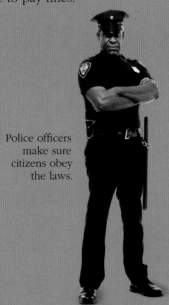

Police officers make sure citizens obey the laws.

119

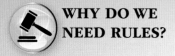

Biography

551 BCE Born in Zou, Lu state, in northeast China.

548 BCE His father dies, and he is brought up by his mother in extremely poor conditions.

532 BCE Marries Qi Quan.

519 BCE Gets a job teaching the sons of a minister in the court of Lu.

501 BCE Begins his career as an administrator.

500 BCE Becomes Minister of Justice of Lu state.

497 BCE After an argument with the duke of Lu, he leaves his homeland to travel around China.

484 BCE Returns to Lu state and devotes himself to teaching.

479 BCE Dies, at the age of 71 or 72.

Good and happy lives

Confucius believed in many traditional Chinese values, such as regard for other people, loyalty, and respect. But he also developed a new system of society, in which the rulers encouraged their subjects to live good and happy lives. His ideas were not generally used in his lifetime, but later Chinese society was based on a system known as Confucianism.

Confucius

"He who learns but does not think, is lost! He who thinks but does not learn is in great danger."

Confucius was one of the most important early Chinese philosophers. His name in Chinese was Kong Qiu, but he was later known as Kong Fuzi, which means "Master Kong." He came from a poor family, but studied hard and became an adviser to the duke of his home state, Lu. It was in this job that he **developed his ideas of how society should be organized**, and how people can lead good and happy lives.

Chinese civil service

In Confucius's time, each region of China was ruled by a noble family. The nobles employed people—civil servants—to advise them and to look after the state administration. Civil servants were chosen for their abilities, not because of the family they were born into. Confucius was made a minister by the duke of Lu because he was a good student.

Young men in China had to study for many years and pass difficult exams to become civil servants.

Spreading the word

When the duke would not take his advice, Confucius left his home state. For about 15 years, he traveled around China, stopping to talk to people in various places. Many were interested in what he had to say, and his ideas slowly spread across China. When he returned home, he devoted the rest of his life to teaching his philosophy.

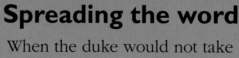

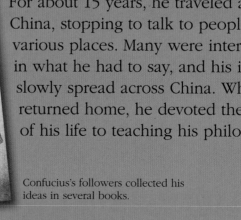

Confucius's followers collected his ideas in several books.

Leading by example

It was traditional in China for rulers to tell their people how they should live. But Confucius thought that everyone in society should lead good and happy lives. He believed that if you act in a good way, people will imitate you. He argued that rulers should not order their people around, but set them a good example by behaving well themselves.

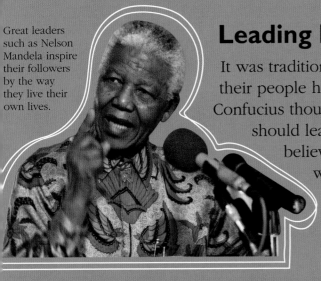

Great leaders such as Nelson Mandela inspire their followers by the way they live their own lives.

Chosen by heaven

In Confucius's time, the Chinese believed that heaven chooses some people to be rulers. It is the job of these rulers to make sure their people live good lives in the way heaven would like. But Confucius thought that all humans, not just the royal and noble families, are chosen by heaven. We can all learn what is right and wrong, and show others how to live well.

Confucius believed that to lead a good life, it is important for people to connect with their community through ceremonies and traditions.

The five constant relationships

According to Confucius, if people behave well toward each other they can live happily together. Society should be organized so that everyone, from ruler to subjects, respects one another. In every relationship, each person must know his or her place and have regard for the feelings of others.

Ruler—Subject
Rulers should be generous, and subjects should be loyal.

Parent—Child
Parents should be loving, and children should be obedient.

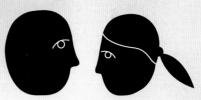

Husband—Wife
Husbands should be good, and wives should be understanding.

Elder child—Younger child
Elder children should be gentle, younger children should be respectful.

Friend—Friend
Older friends should be considerate, younger friends should be polite.

What's the best kind of society?

Throughout history, people have lived in groups or societies. At first these were family groups, which later came together to form tribes, cities, countries, and even empires. Whatever the size of a society, it needs some form of government that will set its rules. **Different societies have different types of government**, ranging from single leaders, such as a king or emperor, to parliaments with hundreds of elected representatives.

Philosopher kings

The ancient Greek philosopher Plato believed that society should be organized so that all its members can lead a good life. However, he thought that most people do not fully understand the things that make a good life, such as justice and virtue. He suggested that the only people who really know about these things are philosophers. So, Plato said, society should be governed by "philosopher kings"—rulers who are also philosophers.

The Roman Emperor Marcus Aurelius (121–180) was also an important philosopher.

Theocracy

Some people believe that it is God, not man, who makes the laws, and society should be governed by the laws of God. Society can be governed on God's behalf by a religious leader or a group of priests. For example, medieval Europe was ruled by the Christian church, and some Islamic states today are governed according to religious laws. This type of society is called a theocracy.

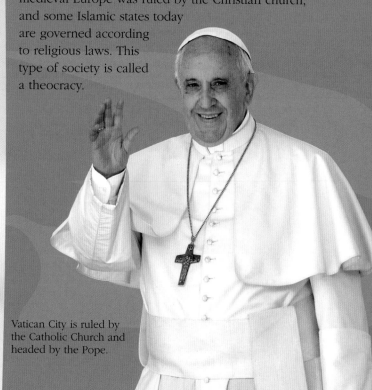

Vatican City is ruled by the Catholic Church and headed by the Pope.

Different types of government

Plato's pupil Aristotle said that the type of society you live in depends on how many people take part in governing it, and whether they govern for the good of society or for themselves. There may be just one ruler, who he called a "monarch" if good, and a "tyrant" if selfish. Or there might be a group of rulers. Aristotle thought the best form of government was what he called a "polity"—a situation where all members of society participate in running it.

Monarchy

For a long time, the most common form of rule was a monarchy, where a country was ruled by a single ruler, such as a king or emperor. Occasionally a monarch is chosen by society, but usually the son or daughter of the existing monarch becomes the next ruler. In many monarchies, people believe that the royal family has been given the right to rule by God.

Monarchs, such as the kings of England, were expected to rule over their people and lead them in battles.

The social contract

In the 17th and 18th centuries, several philosophers questioned the right of monarchs and rich nobles to rule over society. Instead, philosophers such as John Locke said that there should be an agreement—a contract—between the people and the government. In this "social contract," the people give the government the power to make and enforce laws. In return, the government defends its people and protects their rights and freedoms.

Democracy

Today, most countries in the world have some form of government in which all members of society can participate. Such a society—a democracy—is ruled by a government elected by the people. In an election, the people can vote for someone to be their representative, to speak for them and present their point of view. Representatives with the most votes make up the government.

Socialism

French philosopher Jean-Jacques Rousseau (1712–78) argued that society should not be governed by just a few people, but by the "general will" of all its members. His ideas were taken up by German economist Karl Marx (1818–83), who said that people will not be able to rule themselves until they have control of the wealth of their society as well as a say in government. Marx suggested a socialist system, in which all property is owned by the state and administered by a government elected by the people.

Karl Marx

World government

With modern transportation and communications, people today have a more international outlook than ever before. We have begun to create international organizations such as the European Union. There are also truly global organizations, such as the United Nations (UN), that decide conventions on human rights and international laws. Some people believe that one day there will be a world government.

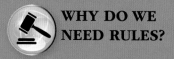
Can society ever be equal?

The American dream
The US was founded on the idea that all people are created equal. Its laws aim to ensure that all its citizens have the same rights and the same opportunities. The "American dream" is that anyone, regardless of family or background, can be successful in life. But the reality is not so optimistic. Although some people have become very wealthy in the US, many others struggle to make a living.

The US is home to some of the richest people in the world, but also to millions of people who live in poverty.

The socialist hope
In the 20th century, many countries, such as Russia and China, tried to create fairer societies by overthrowing their royal rulers and introducing a system called communism. Under communism, everything is owned and run by the state, and every citizen has an equal right to the wealth of the country.

But some leaders and citizens of these countries took advantage of the system to become rich and powerful. Today, only a handful of communist states still exist.

Joseph Stalin (1878–1953) was the all-powerful leader of communist Russia.

The veil of ignorance

In what society would you like to live? If you are rich, healthy, and talented, your answer will probably differ from someone who is poor, sick, or just ordinary. American philosopher John Rawls (1921–2002) came up with this thought experiment to make people think about how society should be organized.

Imagine that before you are born you can choose the society in which you want to live. It could be a society where some people are very poor, but where it is possible to become rich and powerful. Or you could choose a society where people with the most wealth and opportunities contribute more, to help those who have the least. That way, no one is very poor, but no one is very rich either. Before you choose your society, a screen—the "veil of ignorance"—prevents you from seeing your future life. You don't know if you will be rich or poor. You might be healthy, sick, talented, or average. You must choose how to organize your society before you know what kind of life you will have. What type of society would you choose?

In Rawls's thought experiment, for a few people to live in luxury, like this palace in Versailles, many people must live in poverty.

Rich and poor

Throughout history there have been societies in which wealth is very unevenly distributed. During the Middle Ages, for example, rich aristocrats owned almost everything and lived comfortable lives, while peasants owned nothing and worked hard to stay alive. Today, people in Western societies are more equal. However, there are still some countries in the world where there are a few very rich and powerful people, and almost everyone else is poor.

In medieval Europe, peasants worked in the fields and lived in poverty, while a few wealthy people owned the land and lived in castles.

Equality

In some societies, such as Norway, Denmark, and Sweden, almost everyone has a similar standard of living. Doctors and teachers earn only a little more money than farmworkers and sanitation workers, and there are generous welfare benefits for people who need them. But in societies like these, people have to pay high taxes and it is difficult for anyone, no matter how hard they work, to become rich.

In Denmark the majority of people live well, and only a few people are either very rich or very poor.

Think about it

Privilege

Perhaps you think it is right that some people in society have more than others. After all, some people work hard, and others are lazy. Maybe we should reward people who are good at what they do. But is it right that someone from a rich, privileged family has more advantages in life than others? Or that it may be difficult for someone born into a poor family to get out of poverty? Would you choose to create that kiind of society?

What's worse: poverty or inequality?

People often say that money can't buy you happiness. And although no one likes being poor, it's true that poor people can be happy, too. Perhaps what makes people unhappy is when they feel that they are not being treated fairly. Some rich people don't like having too much of their money taken in taxes. And some poor people find it difficult to accept poverty when they see other people living in luxury. Would everyone be happier if we were all equal?

Taking a gamble

Imagine that you have been given $10. You decide not to spend it. Instead, you could buy some lottery tickets with a top prize of $1,000,000. Or you could put it into a savings account, where it will earn a little more money every year. The chances of winning the lottery are very small and, if you lose, your money is gone forever. Investing the money will only give you a little bit more, but you don't lose anything. Why would anybody choose to buy a lottery ticket?

Who makes the rules?

Countries around the world have **different systems for making laws**. Some have just one ruler, a monarch such as a king or queen, or a dictator who has taken control. But most countries are ruled by a government, a group of people who together decide on the laws of the country. In a democracy, the citizens vote in elections to choose the people they want in the government.

Queen Elizabeth II is head of state of the UK, but laws in the UK are decided by elected Members of Parliament.

Rule of royalty

For a long time, nearly every country was led by a king or queen, or an emperor who ruled over several countries. They came from rich and powerful families, and their children became the next rulers. Today, there are still some countries with royal families. However, in most of them there is also a government that decides the laws. Many countries are republics and elect a president instead of having a king or queen.

People's choice

In most countries, it is a basic right for people to have a say in the laws by which they live. They can do this by choosing someone to speak for them—a representative. In a democracy, the citizens vote in regular elections for their representatives. They can choose between several people, who usually belong to political parties with different opinions. The people's representatives meet in a parliament to discuss and vote on new laws.

Power to the people

Some people think that governments do not always make laws that are good for all the citizens. They believe governments make laws to protect rich people but do not help the working people. They say that this is not fair and that everyone should be treated equally in a system known as communism. Communists believe that countries should be ruled by the people, with laws made by the people instead of just the rich minority.

The hammer and sickle symbol represents communism. It was first used during the 1917 Russian Revolution.

Tyranny

Not all countries are ruled with the consent of the people. Sometimes a leader becomes a dictator, someone who decides the laws on his own. Often, a dictator takes power by force, using an army to make people obey his laws. Leaders who rule by making people fear them are known as tyrants. In a country ruled by a tyrant, the people have no say in how laws are made and cannot remove their leader except by force.

Adolf Hitler took power in Germany in the 1930s and became one of the world's most brutal dictators.

SPD
DAS WIR ENTSCHEIDET.

SIE HABEN ES IN DER HAND!

AM 22.09. SPD WÄHLEN.

WWW.SPD.DE

Is anyone above the law?

When countries were ruled by royalty, the king or queen was "above the law." Royal families made the laws but did not have to obey them. Tyrants and dictators think that they are above the law, too. The only way people can remove them from power is through a revolution. In democratic countries, even the leaders have to obey the law. If they don't, they can be arrested and even sent to prison.

These posters let German voters know what their political parties have to say.

127

How do we make laws fair?

Every society, however it is ruled, has laws that are made to protect people and their property. But **people respect only those laws that they think are just** and that are fair to everyone. If there is an argument over property, or if someone commits a crime, the law should make it possible for justice to be done. When we make laws, we must consider everybody's rights and freedom, and decide what is just.

The Greek goddess Themis, armed with a sword and scales, often appears as a symbol of justice in courts of law.

Justice

When someone does something that harms us, or takes something that belongs to us, we think that it is wrong—it is unjust. The laws of a society are made to try to prevent people from behaving unjustly. The legal system ensures that criminals who break the law are punished and that stolen property is returned to its rightful owners. But justice can be done only if the laws are just. Deciding what is just is as difficult as deciding what is right or wrong.

Is it fair that even in rich countries some people have to beg for money in the street?

Fairness

Some people think that justice is the same as fairness. The American philosopher John Rawls said that it is unjust that some people are poor while others are rich, because it is not fair. Justice, in his opinion, is about all of us having a fair share. He said we should have laws that make it possible for everyone to have enough of everything to live comfortably, while no one has too much.

Entitlement

Not everyone agrees that justice is all about fairness. We might think it unfair that a rich man lives in a big house with servants, when someone else lives on the streets. But is this unjust? Robert Nozick (1938–2002) argued that justice is about entitlement—what we have a right to—rather than fairness. If someone sells or gives something to us, it belongs to us. We can sell it, or give it away, but if it is taken away from us, that is unjust.

It wouldn't be just to take away a rich man's house, even if we think it's unfair for him to have so much wealth.

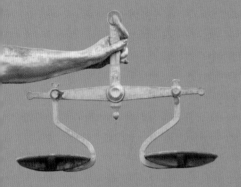

Celebrities such as movie stars are often highly paid, but do they deserve more money than, say, a teacher?

Equality

It is often said that the laws are the same for all, but some people argue that this is untrue. They see the laws as being more in favor of rich and powerful people than of poor people. So is the answer to create a more equal society? For example, we could make it the law that everyone earns the same amount of money. But don't some people deserve more? What about those who do dangerous jobs, such as firefighters, or those who study for years, like doctors? Maybe the answer is to agree that people are not all the same, but to make sure that everyone has the same opportunities.

The law in action

Crime and punishment

In addition to making the laws, we also have to think about what to do with people who break them. Each society has courts of law to decide if someone is guilty of a crime. If a person has taken something that belongs to someone else, the court can make him or her pay it back. The court can also sentence criminals to prison, to perform some form of community service, or to pay a fine. Most people consider punishing criminals as justice to stop them from doing it again, and to discourage other people from committing crimes. The punishment must fit the crime. If it is too harsh or too mild, it could be considered unjust.

People who are held in prison may be given work to do while they are there.

Law enforcement

We have police forces and courts to enforce the law and bring criminals to justice. But can we be certain they do their jobs fairly? How can we make sure the law is enforced in the same way for everyone? Some countries set up special groups to make sure that their police officers and courts do their jobs fairly and treat everyone equally.

Communities *matter,* *not* individuals

All of us are part of a wider group of people—a community. Throughout our lives **we do not act just as individuals but as members of the community**. Communities provide us with all kinds of things, from friendship and support to important services, such as health care and education. We can contribute to our communities in a number of ways, including helping others, working, paying taxes, and volunteering.

A social animal

The ancient Greek philosopher Aristotle wrote that human beings are "social animals" who choose to live in groups or communities. There are many different kinds of community, of which we all belong to more than one. Most of us are part of a family group, a local community, such as a city or village, and a country or state. We are also all members of the vast global community of humans.

Desert-dwelling Bedouin nomads recognize several different types of family group. A group of families form a clan, then several clans form a tribe.

Public goods

British philosopher John Locke thought that one of the jobs of a government is to do things for the good of the public. By raising taxes, communities can provide all kinds of things, from police forces to street signs, which individual people could not provide on their own. These benefits are known as public goods, because everyone can benefit from them whether they pay taxes or not.

Street lighting is a public good that is used by all people.

Welfare

Communities can help people who are in need. Services include health care, elder care, and welfare benefits that help low-income people. These services can be provided by the state, charities, family members, or individuals. Some people believe that the state should provide most of these welfare benefits, and that they should be paid for by taxes. Others feel that welfare should be provided by charities and volunteers, and not by governments.

Welfare activities by charities, such as feeding the homeless, make an important contribution to society.

Community service

Many people help contribute to their communities by doing unpaid work to help others in need, by giving to charity, or by getting involved in politics. Some types of community service are done by choice. Others, such as taking part in a jury at a criminal trial, you have to do if asked. Philosophers called communitarians believe that it is very important for individuals to take an active part in the community.

Taking advantage

One of the problems with community benefits is that some members will try to take advantage of them without paying their share of the cost. For example, some people avoid paying their taxes, and others claim welfare benefits they are not entitled to. Scottish philosopher David Hume (1711–76) said that it is difficult to make everyone contribute, and there will always be some people who try to avoid their responsibilities. But would the unjust actions of a few be a good reason to stop providing the benefits to the majority who need them?

Taking part in activities such as recycling is one way in which everyone can help the community.

Whose life *is it* anyway?

Societies make rules and laws so that people can live their lives without being harmed. But some laws stop us from doing things we want to do, even when they don't seem to harm anyone else. Sometimes the law takes away some of our individual freedom for the good of society as a whole, or to prevent us from harming ourselves.

Should society tell us how to live our lives?

No one tells me what to do!

The philosopher John Stuart Mill (1806–1873) believed that people should be free to do whatever they want, so long as they do not harm others or prevent others from doing what they want. Many people agree that society should not tell us how to think and behave. But different societies have different rules. Some schools, for example, allow children to wear what they like. Others make pupils wear uniforms. In the same way, some governments give people freedom to do things without interference, but others make laws that restrict individual freedom.

Education

When we make laws, we have to find a balance between the things we think people should be allowed to do (their rights), and the things they must do (their responsibilities). Is education a right or a responsibility? In many countries, it is the law that children must go to school. Some children feel that schooling is something they have to put up with, rather than something they really want to do. There are also places where girls are not allowed to go to school, or where there are no schools at all. Don't all children have the right to an education?

Malala Yousafzai from Pakistan campaigns for girls' rights to learn. She was awarded the Nobel Peace Prize in 2014.

Public health

With modern medicines we can prevent people from catching many serious diseases. We can stop infections from spreading, and even get rid of them completely, improving public health. However, disease-fighting programs won't work unless everyone has the vaccinations that give them protection. Should it be made law that every child must be vaccinated against, for example, measles and mumps? What about putting medicine into the public water supply so that everyone gets a dose?

Traffic safety

Thousands of people are hurt in car accidents every day. We know that roads can be dangerous, but there are things we can do to protect ourselves against injury. We can use a seat belt in the car, for example, and wear a helmet and high-visibility clothes when we are cycling. In some countries, it is against the law not to use these safety measures. But if you have a bike crash and you are not wearing a helmet, you are the person who gets hurt. Isn't it up to you to decide whether to wear a helmet or not? On the other hand, why should you object to being told to do something that you know is sensible?

Banning drugs

We all know that smoking cigarettes is harmful. Smoking in public is banned in many countries, so should we make smoking illegal everywhere? Cigarettes are a type of drug and many drugs are illegal. A ban would save lives and money spent on health care. Then perhaps we should ban other dangerous things, such as extreme sports. Is it wrong to tell people what is good or bad for them?

Euthanasia

Almost everyone agrees that killing people is wrong. But what about "mercy killing," which is also known as euthanasia? If a man is on a life-support machine, unconscious, with no chance of ever recovering, would it be wrong to switch off the machine and let him die? What about people who are in constant pain, or who cannot do anything without help? If they don't want to continue living, should a doctor help them end their lives?

Is it **right to censor** *things?*

No one can stop you from thinking what you like. But in many places in the world, **people are not allowed to say what they think**. Some countries censor their newspapers and television stations, stopping them from reporting things they don't want the public to know. Most people think they have a right to say and hear what they choose. But that means we have to let people say things that we don't agree with, or that hurt other people.

Freedom of speech

Philosophers such as Voltaire (1694–1778) and John Stuart Mill (1806–73) argued that in a civilized society, everyone has a right to freedom of speech—they should be allowed to say what they like. That also means that people have the right to write what they want in newspapers and books, and everyone should be allowed to read them. They believed that all censorship is wrong.

People sometimes burn books to show how much they disagree with the ideas in them.

Where do we draw the line?

Even in countries where freedom of speech is considered to be a right, it is against the law to say or write some things, such as lies that will harm other people. But it is not always easy to tell what is the truth, and what is someone's opinion. Should we prevent people from saying or writing something just because we disagree with them? Where do we draw the line?

Why can't I watch R-rated movies?

Most countries have rules to stop young people from watching films that adults consider unsuitable for them. For example, some movies tell stories that may be frightening, or they may contain violence or swearing. Stopping children from seeing these movies is often to protect them from images that they would find disturbing. It also aims to stop children from thinking that bad behavior is normal or acceptable. But who decides what we can and can't watch? Aren't these films harmful for adults, too?

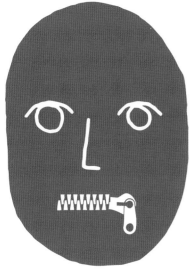

Causing offense

We all like to think we enjoy jokes, but it can hurt when someone pokes fun at you when you don't want them to. Jokes or comments about someone's gender, race, or disability are particularly offensive. Should there be a law against causing offense to others?

Should people have the right to say anything they like, even if it might upset other people?

Freedom of the press

Many journalists believe that they should have the freedom to report news without being censored. They say that the public has a right to know what is happening in the world. But even politicians and movie stars have a right to keep some things private. Which is more important: the freedom of the press, or our right to privacy?

Some photographers—the paparazzi—follow celebrities everywhere and expose their private lives to the public.

Official secrets

Keeping it quiet
One of the jobs of the government of a country is to protect its people. To do this, the country must have armed forces. To prevent people from attacking the country, some of the work the government does, such as military plans, must be secret. The government makes laws to say what things should be official secrets, which only select people can know about. But a bad government could use these laws to hide things they don't want the public to know. How much does the public have a right to know?

Whistle-blowing
People who work for a company or a government are expected to do what they are told by their employers. They have to follow the rules of the organization. Sometimes, though, a person might find out that the organization is doing something that is against the law, or that seems morally wrong. But he has promised not to tell anyone about his work. Should he be a "whistle-blower" and tell the public what the company or the government is doing?

American computer professional Edward Snowden revealed how governments spy on our emails and texts—is he a hero or a traitor?

135

Ask yourself...

Will a good person always be **HAPPY?**

Was I born with **IDEAS** *already* in my head?

HOW can I *tell* if something is **TRUE OR FALSE?**

Could a computer *think?*

Why are some rules **UNFAIR?**

Are *some people* **MORE IMPORTANT** than others?

If I get a new *brain* will I become another *person?*

HOW do I know you're not just a **ROBOT?**

Can I **TRUST** what my eyes see?

Is it always **WRONG** to do something **BAD?**

WHAT is it like to be a *bat?*

Take a turn being a philosopher by asking yourself or your friends these questions. This isn't a test, and you can't be right or wrong. The questions might have lots of answers, or none at all. Just start wondering—that's what philosophy is all about.

What is **THINKING?**

What do we mean by *"good"* and *"bad"*?

WHY should I read about *philosophy?*

How do I know **WHAT IS REAL** and *what isn't?*

HOW do I *know* things?

WHAT is time?

What makes people *happy?*

Do I **CHOOSE** what I *think?*

HOW do I know I *exist?*

Do *animals* **THINK** like we do?

Why can't I do *what I like?*

WHY does *anything* exist?

Glossary

Buddhism The teachings of the Eastern philosopher known as the Buddha, who lived around the 5th century BCE. Buddhists believe that nothing in the world lasts forever and that suffering comes from trying to cling to things that change.

Censorship Banning things such as books, movies, and plays, because parts of them are not considered acceptable for people to read, see, or hear.

Coincidence Two or more things happening at the same time or in the same way, apparently by chance.

Communism A way of organizing society so that everyone belongs to the same social class and all wealth is shared equally among everyone.

Confucianism The system taught by the early Chinese philosopher Confucius. He believed that people can learn about right and wrong by following the good examples of other people.

Democracy A form of government where all people take part in helping to rule a nation by voting for its leaders.

Dialogue A conversation between two or more people, sometimes used as a way of looking at different sides of a philosophical argument.

Dualism The belief that things consist of two separate, different parts. For example, that people are made of both body and mind.

Emotion A feeling, such as love, anger, happiness, or sadness.

Ethics The study of what makes things good or bad.

Existentialism A philosophy that says we are free to choose what we do, and that we must each take responsibility for what we make of our lives.

Feminism The belief that women should have the same rights as men.

Idealism The belief that reality is not made of physical material, but exists only in our minds.

Illusion Something that tricks our eyes and minds, so that what we see isn't what is really there.

Logic Using reasoning to judge whether something is true or false.

Materialism The belief that everything is made of a physical material, including the mind.

Meditation Quiet time spent in deep thought.

Morality The standards we use to decide if an action is good or bad.

Pacifism The belief that using war or violence to settle disputes is always wrong.

Philosophy A word meaning "love of wisdom," which describes various ways of seeking the truth about ourselves and our lives.

Reincarnation The belief that the soul doesn't die when our bodies do but is reborn over and over again, each time in a new body.

Society Any group of people living together in an organized way, in one particular place.

Socratic method Teaching technique used by the ancient Greek philosopher Socrates, who asked one question after another until his students figured out the truth of something for themselves.

Soul Also called the mind or spirit. The part of us we think of as "me," which is capable of feeling and thinking. Some philosophers think the soul is separate from the body and will live forever.

Stoicism Ancient Greek philosophy based on the idea that we should calmly accept whatever happens in life.

Thought experiment An imaginary situation made up to show how a philosophical theory might work out.

Universe In philosophy, the universe, the world, and the cosmos all mean "everything there is."

Utilitarianism The idea that we should aim to do things that bring the greatest good to the greatest number of people.

Virtue The quality of doing something that is morally good.

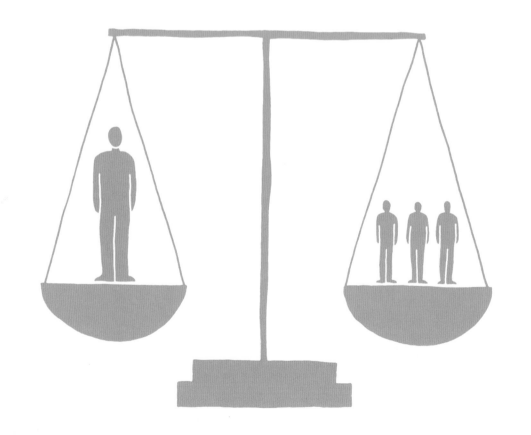

Index

A

Academy (Athens) 22
actions
  and god 47
  and nature 47
  and consequences 92–5, 99
  responsibility for 90, 100, 101
admitting wrong 99, 103
advantage, taking 131
afterlife 63
air 12, 13
Al-Ghazali 46
Alcibiades 18
Alexander the Great 26, 60
the American Dream 124
amnesia 49
Anaximander of Miletus 12
Anaximenes 12
animals
  ethics 110–11
  and feelings 71
  as food 89, 110, 111
  humans and 71, 110–11
  instincts 111
  and language 67
Anselm 20
answers, searching for 9
arguments
  infinite 85
  reasoning and 68–9
Aristotle 13, 14, 15, 20, 22, 26–7, 43, 83, 84, 122, 130
artificial intelligence 72
Avicenna 44–5

B

Babbage, Charles 71
beetle in the box experiment 77
behavior 54, 101, 121
beliefs
  and experience 30, 32
  and knowledge 32
Bentham, Jeremy 93
Bergson, Henri 16
Berkeley, Bishop 47
blind people, dreaming 79
body
  and brain 48–9
  and death 62, 63
  existence of 47
  and mind 41, 42, 44, 45, 46–7, 48–9, 58–9, 63
  right to control own 53
  and soul 43, 46, 58
brain
  and body 48–9
  cells 43
  in a jar 39
  as machine 43, 73
  and processing information 29
  Shoemaker's brain experiment 48
Buddhism 56–7, 58, 59

CD

Camus, Albert 91
cause and effect 50
causes
  final 43
  four 27
censorship 134–5
chance 32, 33
change 23, 57
  and life 31
  of parts 60–61
  personal 42
  and the self 58
  and truths 31
charity 131
children, protecting 134
Chinese Room experiment 72–3
choice
  ethical dilemmas 95, 102–3
  freedom of 100–101
Chomsky, Noam 67
Christianity 63, 88, 100, 114
Christina, Queen of Sweden 40
citizenship 104
civilization 118
class system 124, 125
climate change 109
clones 61
coincidence 33
color 28–9, 53
common sense 44
communication 66–7, 74–5
communism 119, 124, 127
communitarians 131
communities 130–31
computers 70–73
conclusions 68, 69
conflict resolution 115
Confucius 120–21
consciousness 61, 79
consequences 93, 94
copies, of Forms 24, 27
creation 21
crime 129
Darwin, Charles 71, 110
de Beauvoir, Simone 105, 106–7
de Gouges, Olympe 104
death
  euthanasia 133
  life after 62–3
  and soul 46
decisions
  difficult 102–3
  freedom of choice 100–101
  right and wrong 94–5
deduction 68
democracy 123, 126
Democritus 13
Descartes, René 38, 39, 40–41, 42, 50, 71
desires, satisfying 80
determinists 101
Dionysus 22
doubt 38, 39, 57
dreams/dreaming 35, 78–9
drugs 133

E

Earth 13
education, right to 105, 132
effect
  cause and 50
  judging by 31
emergency aid 112
Empedocles of Acragas 13
enlightenment (Buddha) 57
Enlightenment, Age of 52
entitlement 129
environmental ethics 89, 108–9
Epicurus 62, 80, 93
equality
  animal 111
  human 107, 119, 124, 125, 129
  men and women 104–5
ethical dilemmas 95, 102–3
European Union 123
euthanasia 133
evidence 84
evil 82, 83
evil demon 38, 39
example, leading by 121
existence 14, 15, 17, 20, 24–5
  of the body 47
  individual 38–9, 44, 45
  main reason for 43
  and thought 39
existentialism 90–91, 107
experience
  and beliefs 30
  and dreams 78, 79
  and knowledge 97
  and language 75, 77
  learning from 32, 50, 51
  of the world 53
experience machine 81
extinction 111

FG

fairness 128
feelings 42–3, 54, 55
  animals 110
  and dreams 78, 79
  happiness 80–81
  hurting people's 98, 99
  machines 43, 71, 73
  suffering 82–3
feminism 104–5, 106–7
fire 13
Flying Man experiment 44
Foot, Philippa 94–5
foreign aid 112–13
Forms
  perfect 23, 24
  and shadows 24
four causes 27
free will 100–101
freedom
  personal 106–7, 119, 132–3
  of the press 135
  of speech 134
gambling 125
Gandhi, Mahatma 80
Gautama, Siddhartha 56–7
Gettier, Edmund 32
ghost in the machine 71
God
  and change 21
  as creator 21, 83
  existence of 15, 20–21
  and free will 100
  greatness of 20
  judgment by 63
  law of 88
  and suffering 83
  and thoughts/actions 46, 100, 101
good
  and bad 88, 92–3, 118–19
  and evil 82
  meaning of 19
government
  and defense of state 135
  and law 88, 119, 126, 127
  and responsibility for aid 113
  types of 122–3
Greeks, ancient 8, 12–15, 18–19, 22–3, 26–7, 60, 62, 63, 80, 81, 84, 93

HI

Halley, Edmund 41
hallucinations 35
happiness 57, 80–81, 82, 83, 120, 121, 125
  pursuit of 93
harm principle 93
heaven 63, 121
Heidegger, Martin 91
Heraclitus 13
Hinduism 63
Hitler, Adolf 127
Hobbes, Thomas 35, 47, 118
Hollerith, Herman 71
human nature 118–19
human rights 53, 104–5, 128, 132
humans, and animals 71, 110–11
Hume, David 51, 69, 131
Husserl, Edmund 90
Ibn Sina *see* Avicenna
idealism/Idealists 25, 30
ideas
  and life after death 62
  linking 51
  origin of 50–51
  and reality 25, 62
identity, personal 61
illusions 25, 34, 35, 71, 100, 101
imagination 44, 45, 78
individuals
  versus communities 130–31
  see also self
infinite regress 85
infinity 83–4
information
  collecting 25
  from senses 35
  processing 29, 72, 73
instructions, following 72, 73
international cooperation 115, 123
Irigaray, Luce 105
Islam 63, 88, 114

Acknowledgments

Dorling Kindersley would like to thank: Alice Bowden for proofreading, Helen Peters for the index, Tannisha Chakraborthy for additional design, Olivia Stanford for editorial assistance, Maltings Partnership for artworks, Chhaya Sajwan, Pooja Pipil, and Supriya Mahajan for design assistance.

The publisher would like to thank the following for their kind permission to reproduce their photographs:

(Key: a-above; b-below/bottom; c-center; f-far; l-left; r-right; t-top)

6 Corbis: Pasmal / Amanaimages (cla). **Getty Images:** Digital Vision (bl). **iStockphoto.com:** Ruigsantos (cl). **7 Dreamstime.com:** Diamantis Seitanidis (cl). **iStockphoto. com:** Arquiplay77 (cla). **8-9 Corbis:** Laurence Mouton / PhotoAlto (bc). **Dreamstime.com:** Dmitri Rumiantsev. **10-11 Corbis:** Pasmal / Amanaimages. **12 Corbis:** Michael Durham / Minden Pictures (cr). **Getty Images:** Alessandro Contadini / E+ (br, bl, cra). **Photoshot:** World Illustrated (clb). **13 Corbis:** Patrick J. Endres / AlaskaPhotoGraphics (cla). **Getty Images:** Alessandro Contadini / E+ (tl, clb, tr, cr, br); Leemage / Universal Images Group (ca). **14 Corbis:** Isaac Lane Koval (br). **Getty Images:** UniversalImagesGroup (cl). **14-15 Science Photo Library:** Henning Dalhoff (c). **16 The Library of Congress, Washington DC:** LC-DIG-ggbain-38388 (cl). **16-17 Dorling Kindersley:** National Railway Museum, India (c/ Train). **Dreamstime.com:** Manuel Fernandes / Tinoni (b). **17 Corbis:** Mark Garlick / Science Photo Library (b). **Dorling Kindersley:** National Music Museum (tc). **Dreamstime.com:** Hannu Viitanen (cla). **Fotolia:** Gail Johnson (cb). **18 Alamy Images:** Zev Radovan / BibleLandPictures (tc). **Glowimages:** Fine Art Images (b). **19 iStockphoto.com:** Squaredpixels (c). **Photoshot:** World Illustrated (bl). **20 Corbis:** (l). **21 Corbis:** Gerry Ellis / Minden Pictures (cla); Robert Marien (cra). **Getty Images:** Pepifoto (bc); S. Vannini / De Agostini Picture Library (fcra). **22-23 Corbis:** Araldo de Luca (cra). **22 Alamy Images:** Nikos Pavlakis (tc). **23 Alamy Images:** Gianni Dagli Orti / The Art Archive (tc). **Dreamstime.com:** Sharpshot (crb). **24 Glowimages:** Xyz Pictures (tr). **25 Glowimages:** John Lund (cr). **26 Corbis:** Bettmann (tc). **Dreamstime.com:** Nickolayv (bc). **27 akg-images:** Schütze / Rodemann (cra). **Getty Images:** T_kimura / E+ (br). **28 Dreamstime.com:** Mohamed Osama / Midosemsem (bc). **29 123RF.com:** Inesbazdar (bc). **Dreamstime.com:** Mohamed Osama / Midosemsem (crb). **30 Getty Images:** Museum of the City of New York / Archive Photos (br). **Glowimages:** 4x5 Coll / Patrick Byrd (cl). **30-31 123RF.com:** Panithan Fakseemuang (t). **Dreamstime.com:** Sdbower (Smaller balloons). **31 Getty Images:** Steve Pyke / Premium Archive (cr). **Glowimages:** Art Media (bc). **32 Getty Images:** Ascent Xmedia / Digital Vision (cla). **32-33 Corbis:** (c). **34 Getty Images:** Michael Grabois / Moment. **35 Corbis:** KidStock / Blend Images (br); Konrad Wothe / Minden Pictures (tl). **36-37 iStockphoto.com:** Ruigsantos. **38 Dreamstime.com:** Hugo Maes (c). **38-39 Dreamstime.com:** Youths (c). **40 Alamy Images:** GL Archive (tc). **Getty Images:** Culture Club / Hulton Archive (c); Pierre-Louis the Younger Dumesnil / The Bridgeman Art Library (br). **41 NASA:** STS-50. **42 Dreamstime.com:** Jacek Chabraszewski (cl); Zyphyrus (cra). **43 Science Photo Library:** Alfred Pasieka (cra). **44 Getty Images:** De Agostini Picture Library (clb). **44-45 Getty Images:** Sunnybeach / E+ (ca). **45 Dreamstime.com:** Lateci (bl). **46 Dreamstime.com:** Nicholas Burningham (br). Science Photo Library: Oscar Burriel (cl). **47 123RF.com:** Belchonock (c). **Alamy. com:** Zoom-zoom (cra). **Pearson Asset Library:** Tsz-shan Kwok / Pearson Education Asia Ltd (cr). **50 iStockphoto. com:** Suchota (cl). **50-51 Alamy Images:** Lumi Images (c). **51 Corbis:** Michael Bader / Westend61 (crb). **52 Alamy Images:** Alex Segre (tc). **Corbis:** David Bank / JAI (bc). **52-53 iStockphoto.com:** Kenneth Keifer (c). **53 The Library of Congress, Washington DC:** (cr). **54-55 iStockphoto.com:** Asiseeit (c). **55 Alamy Images:** Wonderlandstock (cr). **56 Corbis:** Pascal Deloche / Godong (cla). **56-57 Alamy Images:** Robert Harding

Picture Library Ltd. **57 Dreamstime.com:** Eroticshutter (cr). **58 Dorling Kindersley:** Rough Guides (b). **59 Alamy Images:** Blue Jean Images (br). **Corbis:** Image Source (t). **60 Corbis:** Michael Nicholson (cla). **60-61 Alamy Images:** Alberto Paredes (c). **Dreamstime.com:** Nilsz (Ocean). **61 Alamy Images:** Alberto Paredes (cra). **62 Corbis:** Araldo de Luca (cra). **62-63 Alamy Images:** Victor Paul Borg (b). **63 Alamy Images:** Arkreligion.com / Art Directors & Trip (crb). **64-65 Getty Images:** Digital Vision. **66 Corbis:** Hero Images (b). **67 The Bridgeman Art Library:** French School, (15th century) / Musee National du Moyen Age et des Thermes de Cluny, Paris (clb). **Getty Images:** Karl Ammann / Photodisc (crb); Cultura / Nancy Honey (cra). **Rex Features:** Everett Collection (tc). **68 Alamy Images:** Gianni Dagli Orti / The Art Archive (cra). **Dreamstime.com:** Vitaly Titov & Maria Sidelnikova (crb). **69 Rex Features:** Bournemouth News (clb). **70-71 Alamy Images:** AF archive (b). **71 Corbis:** Imaginechina (br). **Dreamstime.com:** Dny3dcom (c). **Getty Images:** Science & Society Picture Library (cra). **TopFoto.co.uk:** Roger-Viollet (bc). **72 Photoshot:** Elliott & Fry / Lightroom Photos (tl). **72-73 Alamy Images:** Merzavka / Yay Media As (c). **Dreamstime.com:** Maglara (Background). **73 Getty Images:** Leon Neal / AFP (tl). **74-75 123RF.com:** Ivan Smuk (b). **74 Corbis:** 13 / Monashee Frantz / Compassionate Eye Foundation / Ocean (cra). **75 Glowimages:** Fine Art Images (crb). **76 Alamy Images:** Gisela Erlacher / Arcaid Images (cl). **Photoshot:** UPPA (tc). **76-77 Wittgenstein Archive, Cambridge:** (b). **78-79 iStockphoto.com:** Wiangya (c). **79 The Bridgeman Art Library:** Private Collection / Photo Christie's Images (cr). **Corbis:** Dominic DiSaia / Blend Images (bl). **80 Alamy Images:** India Images / Dinodia Photos (cl). **SuperStock:** Cusp (cr). **81 Alamy Images:** Moodboard (ca). **Getty Images:** Steve Fitchett / The Image Bank (clb). **82-83 Getty Images:** Yoichi Kamihara / Amana Images. **83 Alamy Images:** Ideal Stock (tl). **Getty Images:** ERproductions Ltd / Blend Images (cr). **84 Alamy Images:** Ewing Galloway (cra). **Dreamstime.com:** Martin Green (clb). **85 Getty Images:** John W Banagan / Photographer's Choice RF. **86-87 iStockphoto.com:** Arquiplay77. **88 Alamy Images:** Peter Horree (cl). **88-89 Glowimages:** Yvan Travert (c). **89 Corbis:** Bettmann (cra). **iStockphoto.com:** Lovleah (cb). **90 Corbis:** Adoc-photos (bc). **Glowimages:** SuperStock (c). **91 Alamy Images:** Gianni Dagli Orti / The Art Archive (crb). **Dorling Kindersley:** Science Museum, London (cra). **Getty Images:** Gabriel Olsen / FilmMagic (clb). **92 Alamy Images:** Pictorial Press Ltd (c). **92-93 Getty Images:** Doug Chinnery / Moment. **93 Corbis:** Alfredo Dagli Orti / The Art Archive (crb); 237 / Ocean (c). **Glowimages:** H.D. Falkenstein (cra). **iStockphoto.com:** Trekandshoot (bc). **94 Dreamstime.com:** Gabriela Insuratelu (cl). **96 akg-images:** Emil Doerstling (b). **The Bridgeman Art Library:** German School, (18th century) / Private Collection (tc). **97 Alamy Images:** Library of Congress / RGB Ventures / SuperStock (t). **The Bridgeman Art Library:** German School, (18th century) / Deutsches Historisches Museum, Berlin, Germany / DHM (br). **99 Corbis:** GraphicaArtis (tl); JGI / Jamie Grill / Blend Images (cr). **100 Corbis:** Paul Hardy (br). **101 Getty Images:** Datacraft Co Ltd (ca). **102 Getty Images:** Compassionate Eye Foundation / Robert Daly / OJO Images / Iconica (tr). **iStockphoto.com:** Manley099 (crb). **103 Corbis:** Pete Saloutos (cr). **104 Corbis:** Nyein Chan Naing / EPA (cr). **Dreamstime.com:** Serban Enache (bl). **105 Getty Images:** Ulrich Baumgarten (br). **Glowimages:** Museum of London (tl). **106 123RF.com:** Valery Voennyy (c). **Getty Images:** Francois Lochon / Gamma-Rapho (cla). **Rex Features:** Jack Nisberg / Roger Viollet (tc). **106-107 Rex Features:** Photofusion (cra). **107 akg-images:** Mondadori Portfolio (cra). **Getty Images:** Anadolu Agency (tc). **PENGUIN and the Penguin logo are trademarks of Penguin Books Ltd:** (br). **108 Getty Images:** ChinaFotoPress / Stringer (cra). **109 Alamy Images:** Classic Collection / Shotshop GmbH (c). **Corbis:** Denis Spycher / National Geographic Society (r). **Dreamstime. com:** View7 (cl). **110 Dreamstime.com:** James Elliott (cr); Wangyun (cl). **111 Dreamstime.com:** Laurentiu Iordache (tl); Outdoorsman (cr). **Science Photo Library:** Science Source (crb). **112 Corbis:** Michael Coyne (cla); Javier

Vázquez / Demotix / Demotix (clb). **113 Alamy Images:** John Brown. **114-115 Corbis**. **114 Photoshot:** De Agostini (bl). **Corbis:** Luc Gnago / Reuters (bl). **Getty Images:** Agence France Presse / Hulton Archive (crb). **116-117 Dreamstime.com:** Diamantis Seitanidis. **118 Corbis:** Fred Ward (cl). **118-119 SuperStock:** Iberfoto (c). **119 Corbis:** Image Source (br); Joseph Sohm / Visions of America (tc). **Getty Images:** Dwight Nadig / E+ (cr). **120 akg-images:** British Library (tc); Roland and Sabrina Michaud (bc). **Alamy Images:** The Art Gallery Collection (cr). **120-121 Getty Images:** Christian Kober / AWL Images (b). **121 Alamy Images:** DC Stock (tl). **122 Getty Images:** Vincenzo Pinto / AFP (crb). **123 Alamy Images:** GL Archive (tc). **Corbis:** Bettmann (bc). **124 Alamy Images:** Don Davis (bl). **Corbis:** George Steinmetz (cla). **124-125 Dreamstime.com:** Lenise Zerafa (b). **125 Dreamstime.com:** Ed Francissen (c). **Getty Images:** De Agostini Picture Library (tl). **126 Alamy Images:** V&A Images (cla). **126-127 Corbis:** Julian Stratenschulte / Dpa (b). **127 Rex Features:** (cr). **128-129 Alamy Images:** Jonathan Buckmaster (c). **Dreamstime.com:** Awesleyfloyd (Background). **129 Alamy Images:** ZUMA Press, Inc (cr). **Getty Images:** John Woodworth / E+ (ca). **SuperStock:** Yuri Arcurs Media (c). **130 Glowimages:** Heeb Christian. **131 Alamy Images:** Jim West (cr). **Corbis:** Tim Pannell (bl). **132 Corbis:** Ocean (clb). **Getty Images:** Stringer / AFP (br). **132-133 Dreamstime.com:** Bidouze Stéphane (Background). **134 Getty Images:** Stringer / AFP (clb); Thomas Northcut / Photodisc (c). **135 Alamy Images:** Losevsky Pavel (b). **Getty Images:** Barton Gellman / Getty Images News (crb)

All other images © Dorling Kindersley
For further information see: www.dkimages.com